Sew Felt Animals from Apple Blossom Wood

A PRACTICAL GUIDE TO SEWING HEIRLOOM ANIMAL DOLLS AND THEIR CLOTHING

CLAIRE BOWMAN

DAVID & CHARLES
—PUBLISHING—

www.davidandcharles.com

Contents

INTRODUCTION ... 6

TOOLS AND MATERIALS ... 8

GENERAL TECHNIQUES ... 10

THE ANIMALS ... 14

Bertie Bear ... 16

Eli and Elisha Elephants ... 24

Chester and Sapphire Foxes ... 32

Emma and Byron Highland Cows ... 40

WARDROBE ... 48

Austen Waistcoat ... 49

Classic Shirt ... 50

Classic Trousers ... 52

Shelby Coat ... 54

Peaky Cap ... 56

Horseshoe Waistcoat ... 57

Swallowtail Jacket ... 59

Apron Dress ... 61

Bella Bloomers ... 64

Josephine Jacket ... 66

Harris Jacket ... 68

Berry Brim Hat ... 70

Perfect Petal Jacket ... 72

Mandarin Waistcoat ... 75

Darcy Trousers ... 77

Regency Jacket ... 80

TEMPLATES ... 82

SUPPLIERS ... 118

ABOUT THE AUTHOR ... 118

ACKNOWLEDGEMENTS ... 118

INDEX ... 119

INTRODUCTION

Hello and welcome to Apple Blossom Wood – a magical woodland full of animals who are always happy and eager to help one another. It all started when I had the idea of making a tiny little bear – but as I was designing my Bertie Bear, he turned into a stylish gentleman bear. I enjoyed making him so much! He stood looking at me in my studio for a week and I just knew he had to have friends, so the next 18 months became a wonderful journey and Apple Blossom Wood came to life. I have now designed and made over 50 animals and still have a huge list of animals I want to make!

In this book, you will find seven of the animals who live there. Each animal has its own authentic style from a bygone age. Every piece of clothing has been meticulously designed and tailored. At the back of the book there is a whole wardrobe of interchangeable clothes so that you can create your own twist on their look. I can't wait to see all of your creations !

Claire xx

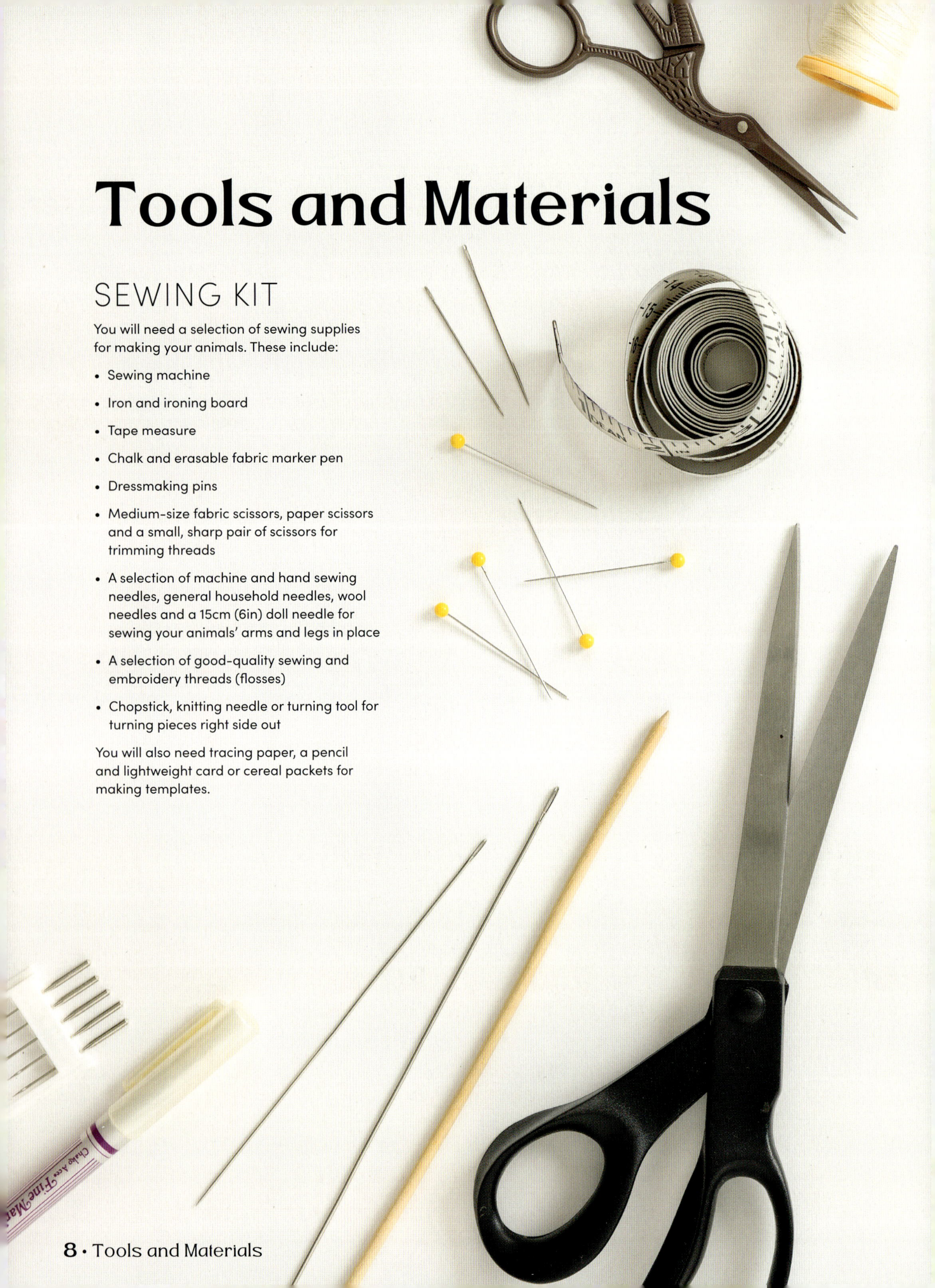

Tools and Materials

SEWING KIT

You will need a selection of sewing supplies for making your animals. These include:

- Sewing machine
- Iron and ironing board
- Tape measure
- Chalk and erasable fabric marker pen
- Dressmaking pins
- Medium-size fabric scissors, paper scissors and a small, sharp pair of scissors for trimming threads
- A selection of machine and hand sewing needles, general household needles, wool needles and a 15cm (6in) doll needle for sewing your animals' arms and legs in place
- A selection of good-quality sewing and embroidery threads (flosses)
- Chopstick, knitting needle or turning tool for turning pieces right side out

You will also need tracing paper, a pencil and lightweight card or cereal packets for making templates.

FABRICS

FABRICS FOR THE ANIMALS

All animals are made from wool felt (30% wool, 70% acrylic). I really don't recommend using anything else – fabrics with no give, such as cotton, don't work, as they just don't take the shape of the animals, especially their heads. I use marl wool felt, which is a blend of colours that gives a textured look. I much prefer it to plain wool felt.

The Highland cows also have fur on their heads that is sewn on afterwards by hand. For this, use a foxy deluxe 60mm (2½in) pile fur. You need to exercise a little more care when sewing faux fur. When cutting out, place the templates on the back of the fabric, with the fur pile running in the direction indicated on the templates, and draw around them. Only cut the fur fabric from the back, making tiny snips through the pile close to the backing fabric. Pull the templates and fabric apart gently. When pinning the fur pieces together, try to push as much of the fur as possible into the centre, away from your drawn lines. After you have sewn your seams, gently use either a pin or a comb to tease all the fur at the seams to the right side.

FABRICS FOR THE CLOTHES

Choosing the right fabric for the animals' wardrobes can be a deal breaker. Good-quality cotton fabric works well for all the clothes in this book. Light- to mediumweight printed cotton, which is reasonably closely woven, is a good all-rounder. Quilting cottons are the heaviest that can be used.

Think about the scale of any pattern, too: ditsy prints will be in scale with the animals. Lightweight woven fabrics with small checks, herringbone or dogtooth look great for trousers and jackets, while tiny prints such as remnants of Liberty lawn are perfect for feminine-looking dresses.

Another couple of fabrics to think about are pincord and soft cotton flannel – they really look wonderful on the animals. Pincord, also known as pinwale or needlecord, is the finest cord, with a count at the upper end of the spectrum (above 16). The corduroy is coloured or printed with pigment dyes. Flannel is a soft-to-the-touch fabric made from 100% cotton that works really well for the jackets and peaky cap. You can buy printed flannels with small checks and dogtooth patterns that lend themselves to the animals' clothes.

General Techniques

TEMPLATES AND CUTTING OUT

Transfer all pattern pieces onto a piece of lightweight card, as this will be easier to draw around on your fabric. Place the template on your fabric (right sides together, if you are cutting two pieces from your template – for example, a left and a right front). Place each pattern piece so that the grainline arrow runs lengthwise on the fabric, parallel to the selvedge (selvage) edges, regardless of the way the fabric has been folded.

Using an erasable fabric marker pen, draw all around, then transfer any markings such as darts or notches, making sure that all markings are on the wrong side of the fabric.

When you are ready to cut out, add a seam allowance of about 6mm (¼in), unless otherwise indicated on the template. Your seam allowances don't have to be completely accurate, as you will be using the line that you drew around the template as your sewing line. (Why not an accurate seam allowance, you may ask? Surely, the smaller the garment the more accurate you must be. The answer is that using the sewing/drawn line ensures a perfect fit.)

Carefully pin and tack (baste) the pieces together along your drawn line.

SEWING

All the projects in this book are machine sewn. I recommend using stitch length 2, as I find it looks really neat on the animals. If you have the needle-down function on your machine, I recommend that you use it when turning corners or going round curves. Always tie off the threads at the start and at end of a sewn line.

If you prefer, however, you can hand stitch the animals. If you opt to do this, cut the animal templates out on the drawn line, without adding any seam allowances, then blanket stitch them together for a lovely rustic look, following the instructions for the machine-sewn animal. Alternatively, follow the machine-sewn animal instructions (adding seam allowances where indicated), using a small back stitch and sewing on the drawn line. Their clothes can be hand sewn using back stitch and following the machine stitch instructions.

To keep things really neat, you need to deal with the seam allowances as you go. The first thing to do is to trim them: this just means cutting the seam allowances down by about half (so make them about 3mm/⅛in rather than 6mm/¼in) to reduce bulk. For the same reason, it's also a good idea to snip off any corners once you've sewn a seam.

If you've sewn a curved seam, such as a neckline or an armhole, make small snips into the seam allowance. This releases tension in the fabric and enables the sewn line to lie smoothly.

Then you need to neaten the raw edges of the seams, to prevent fraying. Machine zigzag and overlocking are good and quick options, but oversewing by hand is a good choice, too. Another quick-and-easy method is to use pinking shears. For the purposes of the projects in this book, this only applies to the animals' clothes, as felt (which is used to make their bodies) doesn't fray.

Pressing a garment can make it look perfect and you should press after each process. Keeping a mini iron and a small ironing pad close to your machine really helps. Open seams up and press, making sure you set the right temperature for the fabric you are using. Never push or drag the iron over the fabric, as this can distort the grain.

SHAPING

There are various ways of adding shaping to your animals' garments. The most common is to sew darts at the waist of a shirt, jacket, waistcoat or trousers. The darts cinch the fabric in around the waist, creating an hourglass silhouette. They are shown on the templates as a triangle. To sew them, simply fold the fabric right sides together along the outer lines of the triangle and pin in place, making sure the two sides of the triangle align perfectly. Then sew from the widest point of the dart to the tip, alowing the needle to run off the end of the dart rather than backstitching.

Pleats are another way of gathering fabric. These are marked on the templates as vertical lines with arrows in between them. Fold the fabric along the vertical lines in the direction indicated by the arrows, then sew down from the top of the pleat for 3cm (1¼in) or so.

Gathering creates a series of small folds close to the edge of a piece of fabric. It is often used to add fullness to the tops of sleeves, or to skirts. Work two rows of stitching inside the seam allowance, leaving the thread loose at both ends, then gently pull the threads to gather the fabric to the required length and even out the gathers with your fingers. When gathering by machine, always increase your stitch length to 4. When gathering by hand, work two rows of running or gather stitch.

APPLIQUÉ

Appliqué is the technique of adding a second fabric (usually a decorative motif, although it can be used to add pockets, too) to your foundation fabric, to create an embellishment. The name comes from the French word *appliquer*, meaning 'to apply'. Appliqué can be hand sewn or machined in place, usually with blanket stitch. Fusible bonding web is used to prevent fraying and to hold the appliqué piece in position while it is being sewn.

Most modern machines have blanket stitch. Use a small stitch – 1.5 length and 1.5 width. If your machine doesn't have this feature a small zigzag stitch looks great, too. For details of how to sew blanket stitch by hand, see below.

HAND STITCHES

The stitches shown below are simple, decoratives ones that you can easily use to embellish your projects.

BLANKET STITCH

Using three strands of embroidery thread (floss), bring the needle UP at 1. Insert the needle DOWN at 2, a stitch length both to the right and down from the line. In the same motion, come UP at 3, perpendicular to the line. Place the thread under the needle tip and finish pulling the needle to the front of the fabric. Continue along the line.

Blanket Stitch

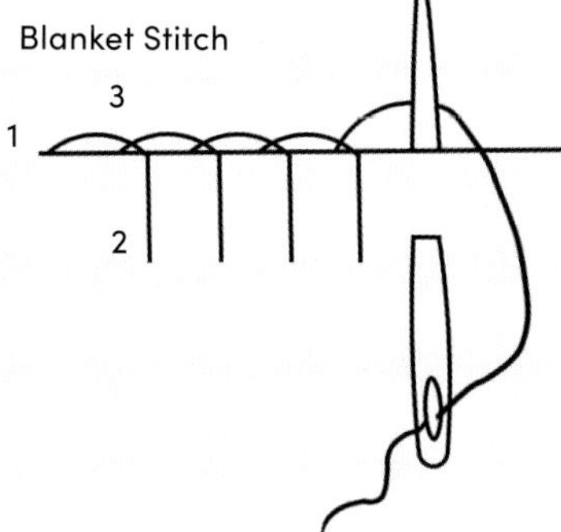

BACK STITCH

To back stitch, bring the needle UP at 1. Insert the needle DOWN at 2, making a stitch backwards along the line to meet the previous stitch. Come UP at 3, a stitch length away from 1. Continue along the line.

Back Stitch

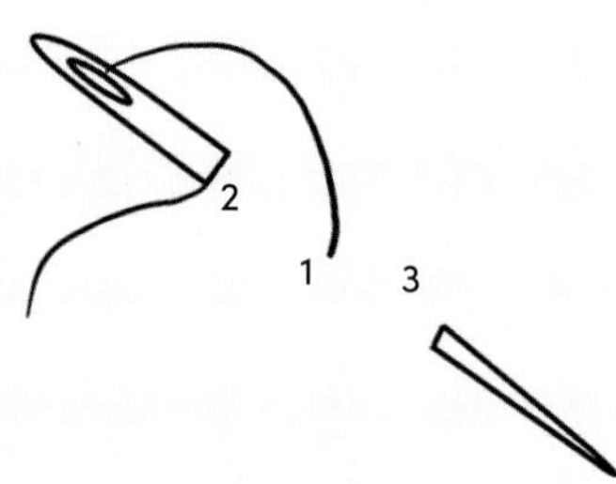

RUNNING STITCH / GATHER STITCH

Take the needle up and down through the fabric at regular intervals, so that both the stitches and the gaps in between them are even.

Running Stitch

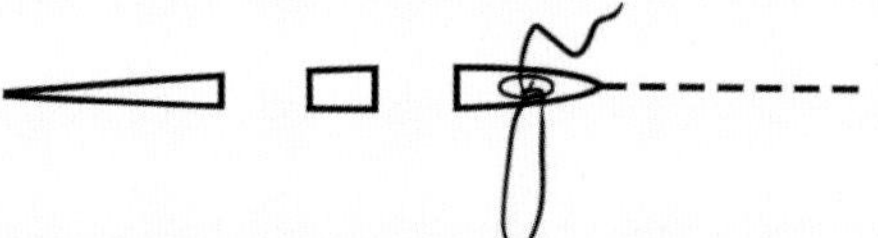

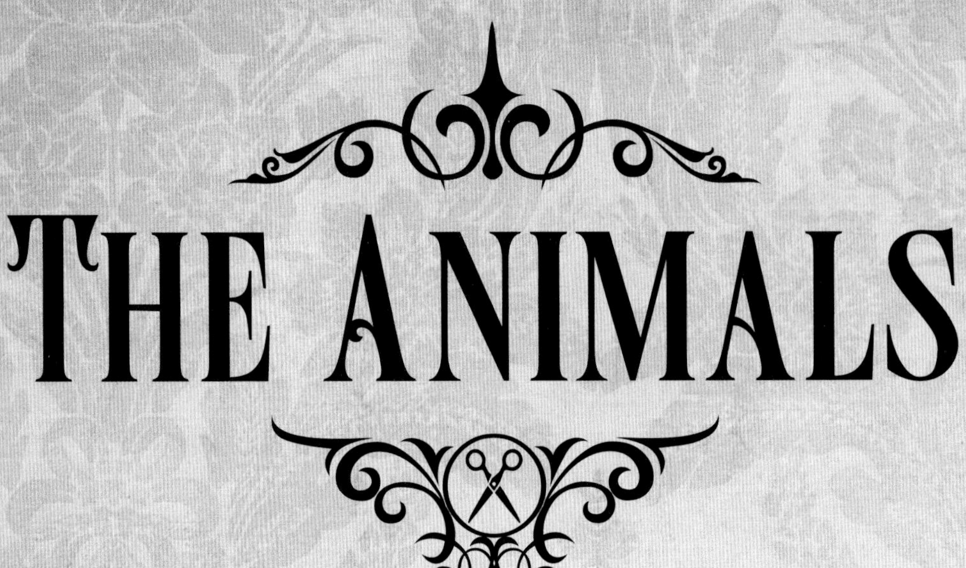

The Animals

This section includes all the information you need to make seven charming characters from Apple Blossom Wood. Once you've mastered the first one (Bertie Bear) you'll have no trouble making the others, as the basic construction is the same – you simply use slightly different templates for the head and facial details to give each animal its individuality. I use marl felt for all the animals: not only does it have a soft, fur-like quality but felt doesn't fray, which takes a lot of the hassle out of sewing!

Each animal has a list of all the materials you will need, along with which templates you need to copy. All the templates are full size, so you won't need to do any tricky maths to work out how to enlarge them. Simple diagrams and written instructions take you step by step through the sewing process. You'll also find a suggested wardrobe for each animal, though of course you can mix and match clothes if you prefer.

Reminder

For a really neat finish, always trim and neaten your seam allowances, and press at every stage of the construction process.

Bertie Bear

Bertie is a very dapper chap. He is the proprietor of Blossom Antique Emporium and spends most of his days in his shop, sorting out the stock. He is an avid collector of grandfather clocks and loves nothing more than bringing them back to life.

BERTIE

You will need

- Universal animal templates: Body, arm, leg
- Bear templates: Side head, head gusset, nose, ear
- 50 x 50cm (20 x 20in) marl beige wool felt for body, head, arms, legs and outer ears
- 5 x 10cm (2 x 4in) small printed cotton fabric for inner ears
- 2.5 x 5cm (1 x 2in) brown wool felt for nose
- 250g (8oz) toy filling
- 2 x 5mm (3⁄16in) black beads for eyes
- Matching sewing thread
- Doll needle 15cm (6in)

FINISHED SIZE: 40cm (16in)

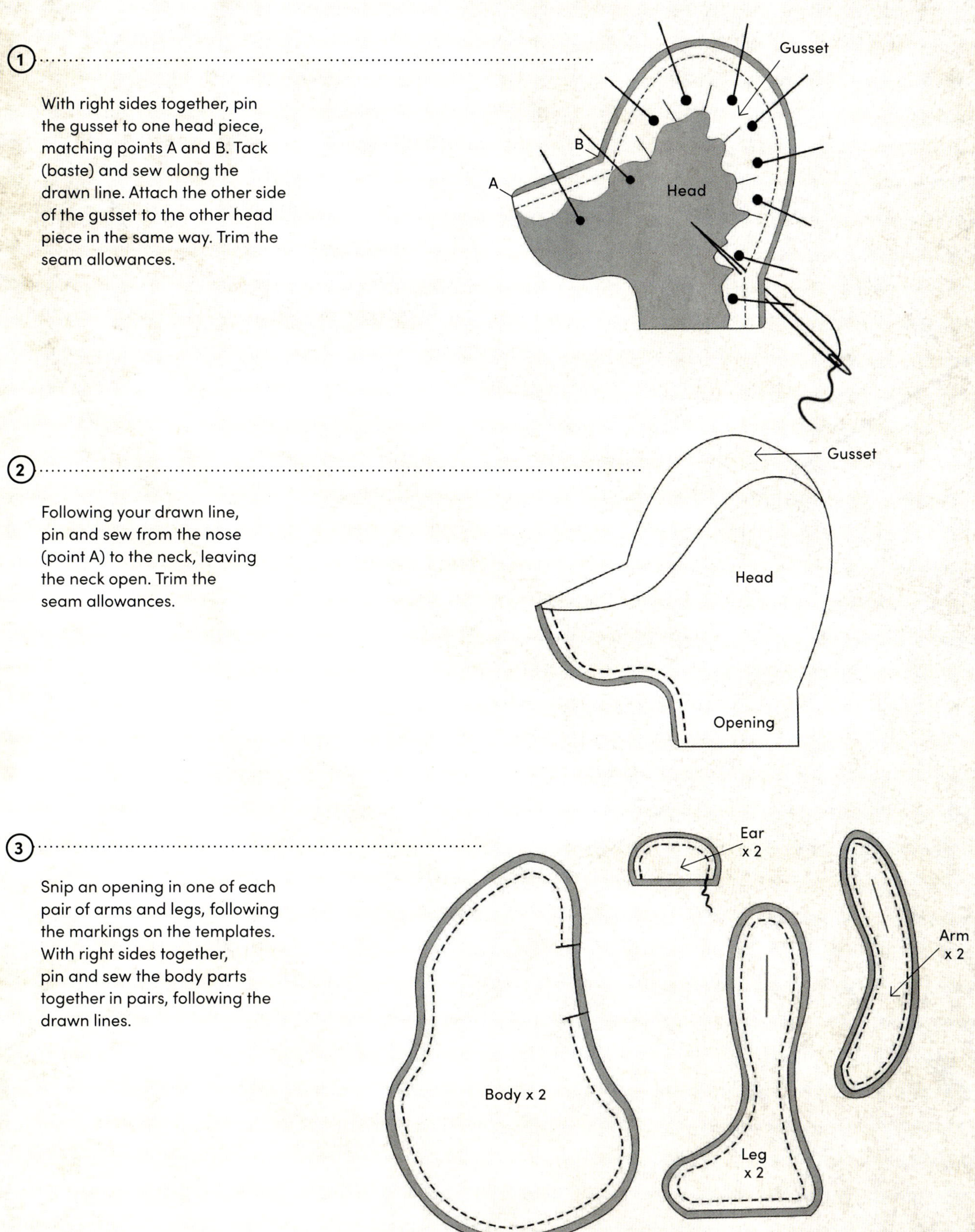
1
With right sides together, pin the gusset to one head piece, matching points A and B. Tack (baste) and sew along the drawn line. Attach the other side of the gusset to the other head piece in the same way. Trim the seam allowances.
Gusset
B
A
Head
2
Following your drawn line, pin and sew from the nose (point A) to the neck, leaving the neck open. Trim the seam allowances.
Gusset
Head
Opening
3
Snip an opening in one of each pair of arms and legs, following the markings on the templates. With right sides together, pin and sew the body parts together in pairs, following the drawn lines.
Ear
x 2
Arm
x 2
Body x 2
Leg
x 2

4

Turn the body parts right side out. Fill the body, arms and legs with good-quality toy filling, adding as much as you can so that the body parts are hard to the touch. Now oversew the openings closed and oversew along the straight edges of the ears.

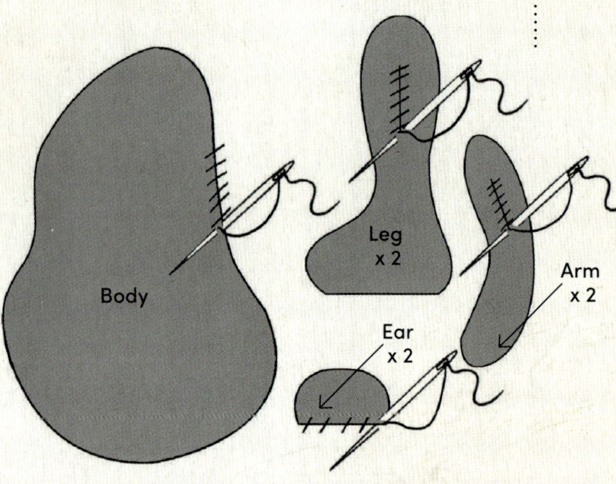

5

Turn the head right side out and fill with toy filling. Gather the neck edge of the head by hand, pull the threads tightly and oversew the edges of the neck together.

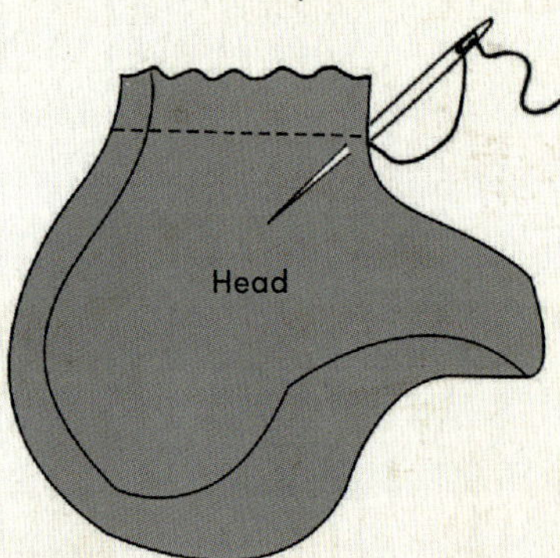

6

Match the centre front seams of the head and body. Insert a large doll needle through the head and body to hold them in position while you oversew them together. I recommend sewing round three times for added security.

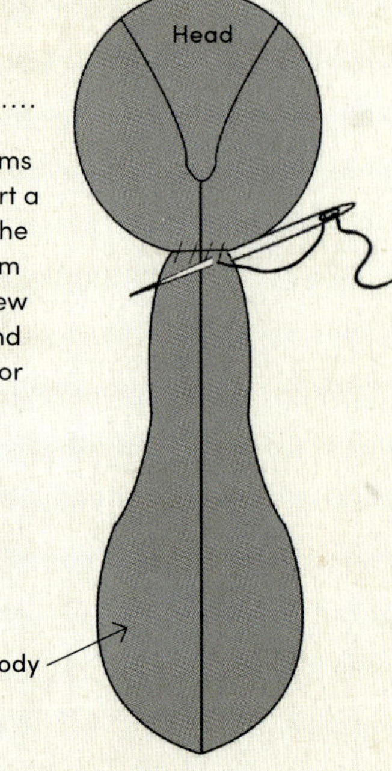

7

Place one arm on either side of the body. When you are happy with their position, use a large doll needle to hold them securely while you sew them in place. Use double thread and a second doll needle, sew back and forth through both arms and body at least ten times, then tie off.

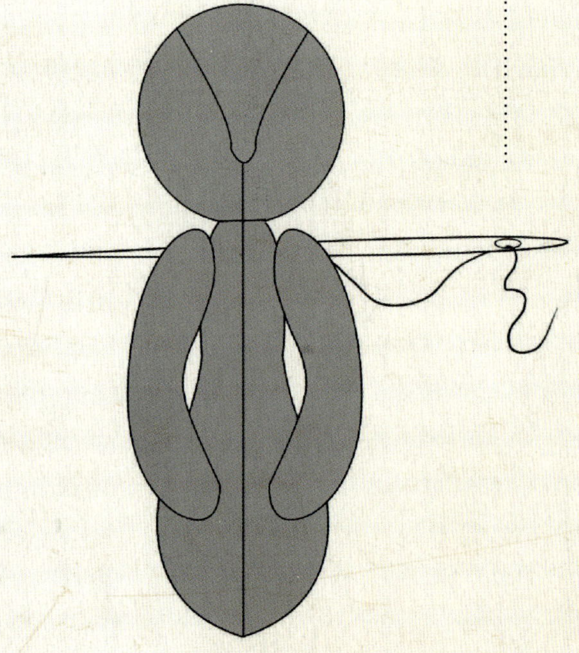

8

Sew the legs in place in the same way as the arms, making sure they are level so that Bertie will be able to stand.

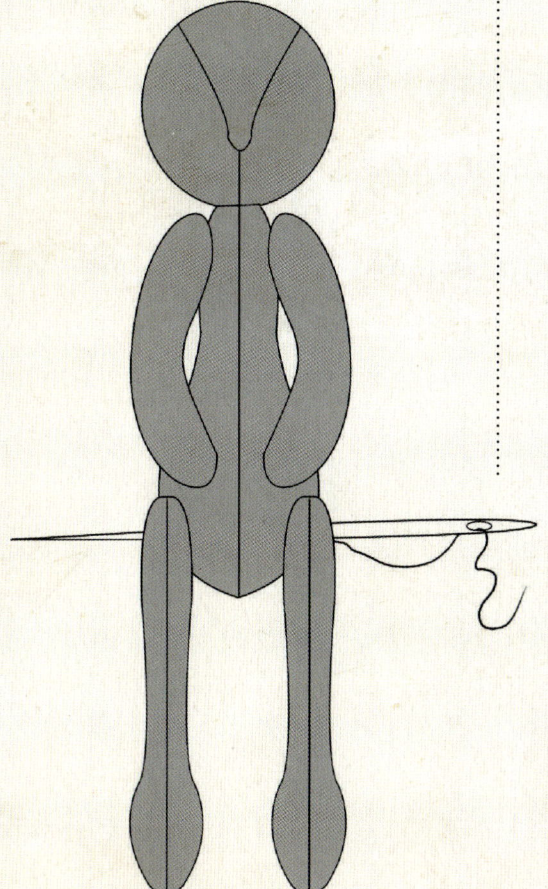

10

Now it's time to make the face. Using pins, place the bead eyes and nose on the face and move them around until you are happy with the position, then sew them on. Do the same thing with the ears, making sure the contrast fabric faces forwards.

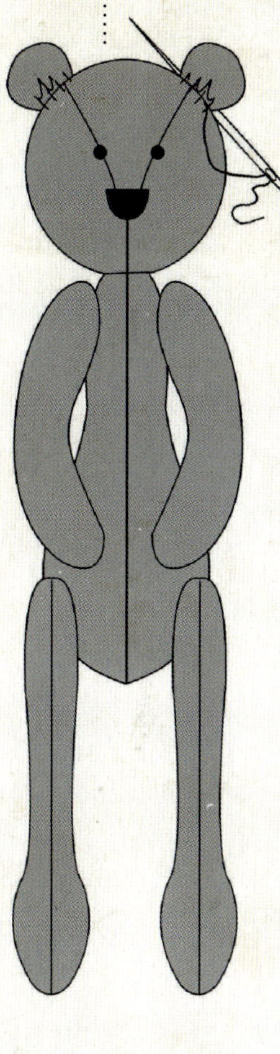

9

Fold the ears in half, making sure the contrast fabric is on the inside, and oversew along the bottom edge.

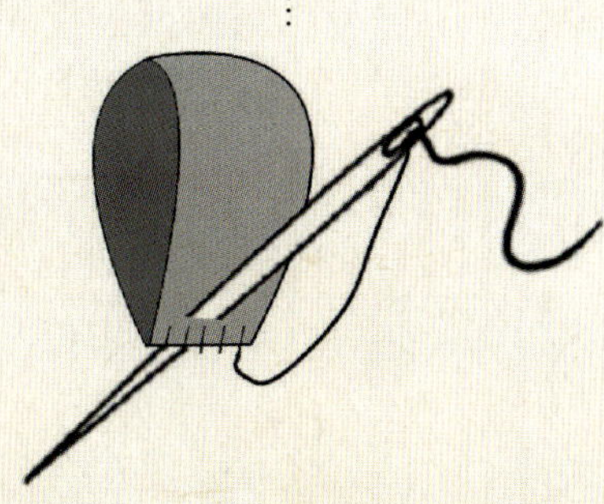

Bertie's Wardrobe

Peaky cap
Shelby coat
Classic shirt

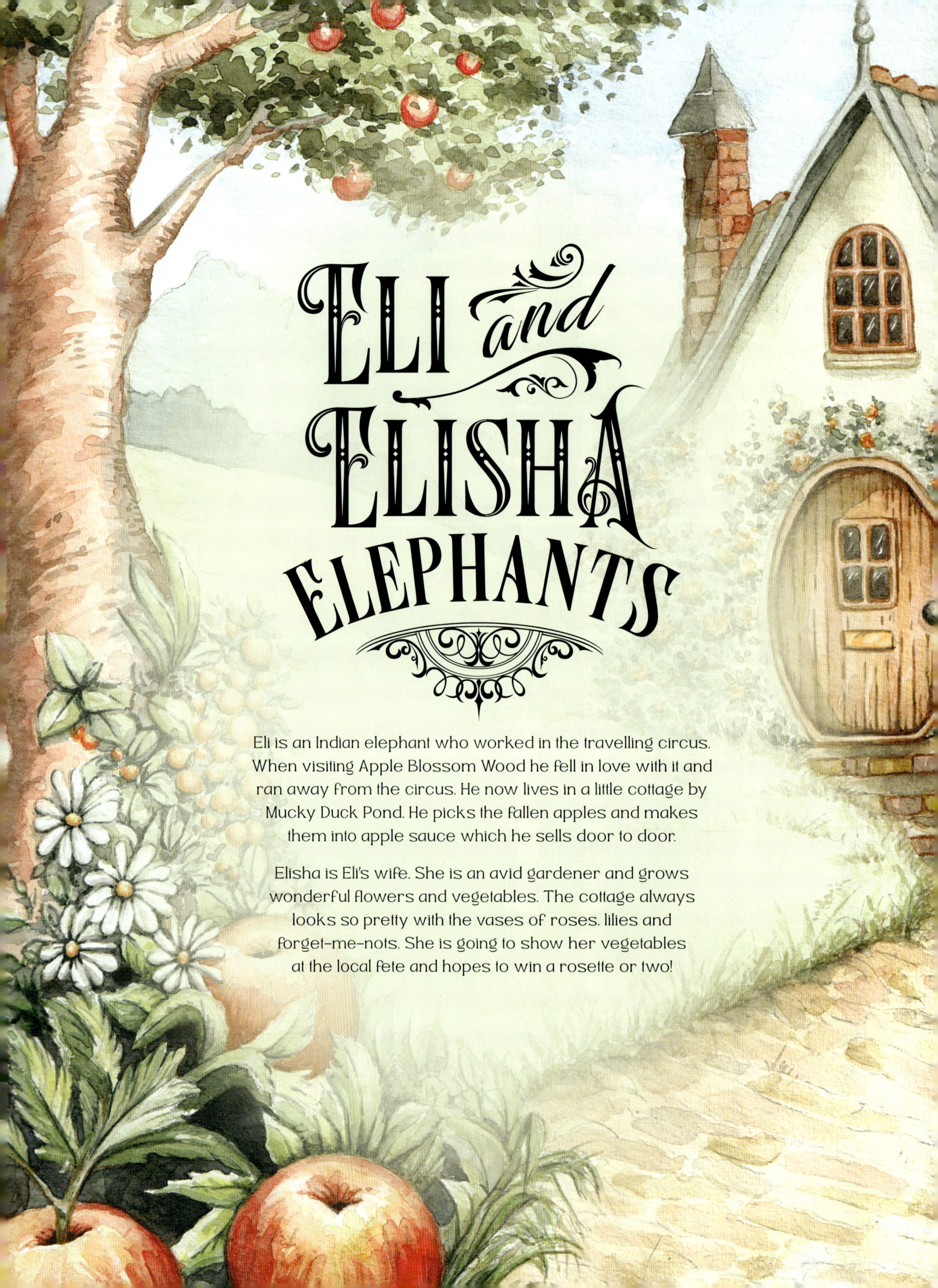

Eli and Elisha Elephants

Eli is an Indian elephant who worked in the travelling circus. When visiting Apple Blossom Wood he fell in love with it and ran away from the circus. He now lives in a little cottage by Mucky Duck Pond. He picks the fallen apples and makes them into apple sauce which he sells door to door.

Elisha is Eli's wife. She is an avid gardener and grows wonderful flowers and vegetables. The cottage always looks so pretty with the vases of roses, lilies and forget-me-nots. She is going to show her vegetables at the local fete and hopes to win a rosette or two!

Eli & Elisha

You will need

- Universal animal templates: Body, arm, leg
- Elephant templates: Side head, head gusset, ear
- 40 x 90cm (16 x 36in) marl grey wool felt for all pieces except inner ears
- 9 x 18cm (3½ x 7in) small printed cotton fabric for inner ears
- 250g (8oz) toy filling
- 2 x 4mm (⅛in) black beads for eyes
- Matching sewing thread
- Variegated machine or stranded embroidery thread (floss)
- Doll needle 15cm (6in)

FINISHED SIZE: 40cm (16in)

All of the animals are made in the same way as Bertie Bear, with some modifications for the heads.

2

Following your drawn line, pin and sew from the front tip of the gusset down the trunk and around to the neck, leaving the neck open. Trim the seam allowances.

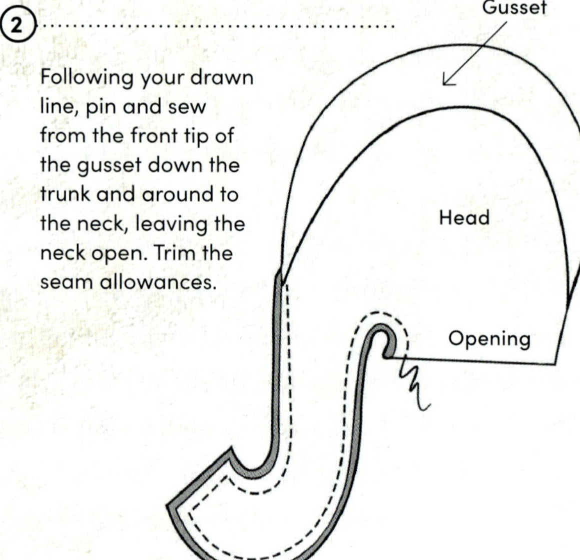

3

Turn the head right side out and fill with toy filling. Gather the neck edge of the head by hand, pull the threads tightly and oversew the edges of the neck together.

Make and assemble the body, arms and legs, following the instructions for Bertie Bear, steps 3–8.

1

With right sides together, matching points A, pin the gusset to one head piece. Tack (baste) and sew along the drawn line. Attach the other side of the gusset to the other head piece in the same way. Trim the seam allowances.

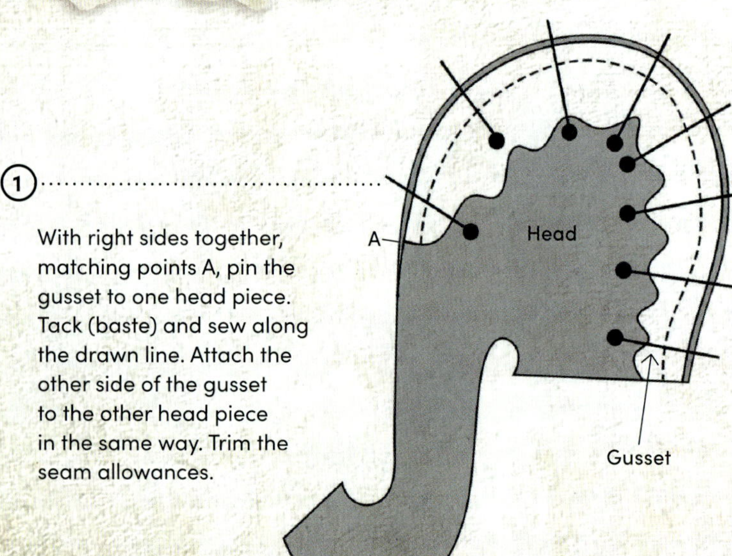

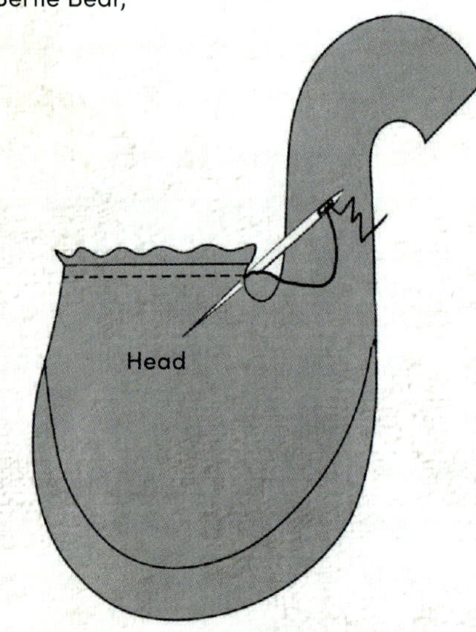

4

With wrong sides together, place a contrast fabric ear on a felt ear. Using variegated machine thread, sew together following the lines on the sewing template. Alternatively, you can sew by hand, using three strands of variegated embroidery thread (floss). Repeat for the second ear. The ears are left raw and you can fray the contrast fabric if you wish.

5

Turn under the straight edges of the ears along your drawn line and oversew together to neaten.

6

Pin the ears on the elephant's head, making sure the contrast fabric faces forwards, and oversew in place front and back. Sew down the trunk, changing the angle and length of your stitches. You can also randomly stitch over some of the seams on the head and body to enhance the wrinkled skin effect. Using pins, place the bead eyes on the face. Move them around until you are happy with the position, then sew them in place.

Eli's Wardrobe

Swallowtail
jacket
Classic
trousers

Elisha's
Wardrobe
Bella
bloomers

Josephine
jacket
Apron
dress

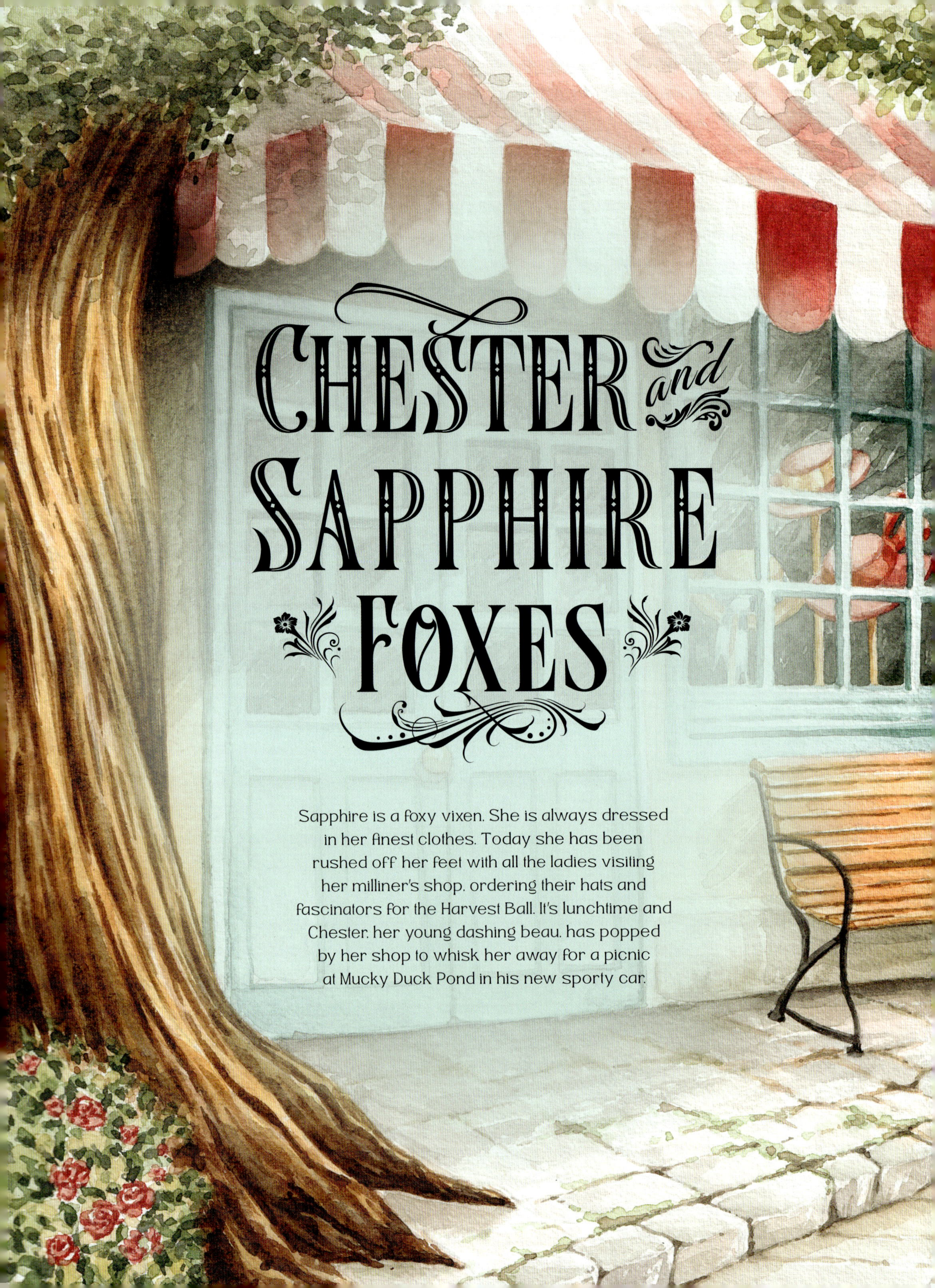

Chester and Sapphire Foxes

Sapphire is a foxy vixen. She is always dressed in her finest clothes. Today she has been rushed off her feet with all the ladies visiting her milliner's shop, ordering their hats and fascinators for the Harvest Ball. It's lunchtime and Chester, her young dashing beau, has popped by her shop to whisk her away for a picnic at Mucky Duck Pond in his new sporty car.

CHESTER & SAPPHIRE

You will need

- Universal animal templates: Body, arm, leg
- Fox templates: Upper side head, lower side head, head gusset, nose, ear
- 50 x 50cm (20 x 20in) marl rust wool felt for body, upper side head, head gusset, arms, legs and outer ears
- 40 x 10cm (16 x 4in) white wool felt for lower side head and inner ear
- 3 x 3cm (1⅛ x 1⅛in) black wool felt for nose
- 250g (8oz) toy filling
- 2 x 4mm (⅛in) black beads for eyes
- Matching sewing thread
- Black stranded embroidery thread (floss) for mouth
- Brown stranded embroidery thread (floss) for whiskers
- Doll needle 15cm (6in)

FINISHED SIZE: 40cm (16in)

All of the animals are made in the same way as Bertie Bear, with some modifications for the heads.

1. With right sides together, pin one upper side head piece to a lower side head piece, lining up the markings at point B. Tack (baste) and sew along the drawn line. Trim the seam allowances. Repeat with the second upper and lower side head pieces.

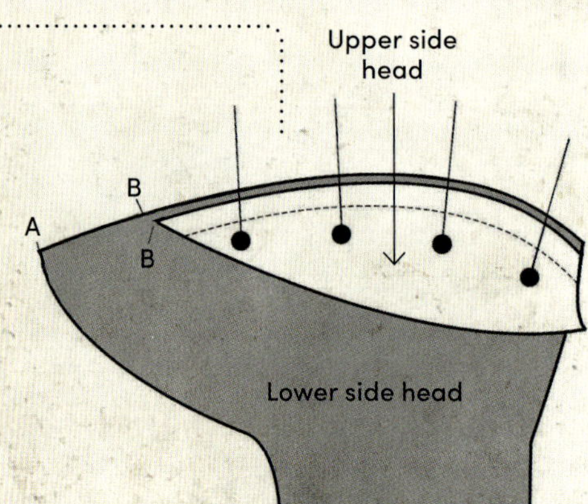

2. With right sides together, matching points A and B, pin and sew the gusset to one head piece, following your drawn line. Attach the other side of the gusset to the other head piece in the same way. Trim the seam allowances.

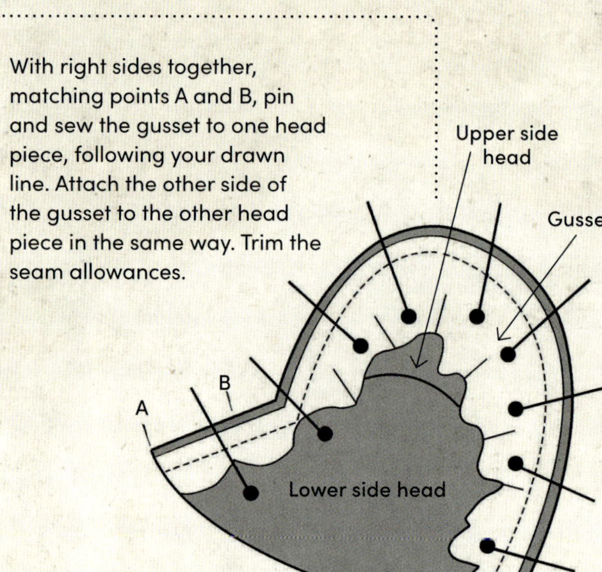

3. Following your drawn lines, pin and sew from the nose (point A) to the neck, leaving the neck open. Trim the seam allowances.

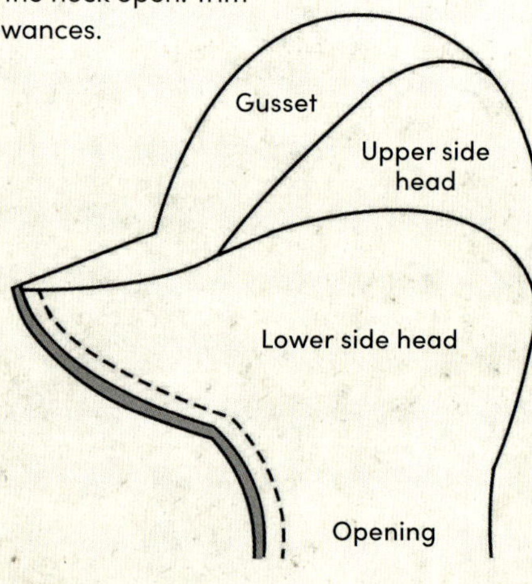

4

Turn the head right side out and fill with toy filling. Gather the neck edge of the head by hand, pull the threads tightly and oversew the edges of the neck together.

Make and assemble the body, arms, legs and ears, following the instructions for Bertie Bear, steps 3–9.

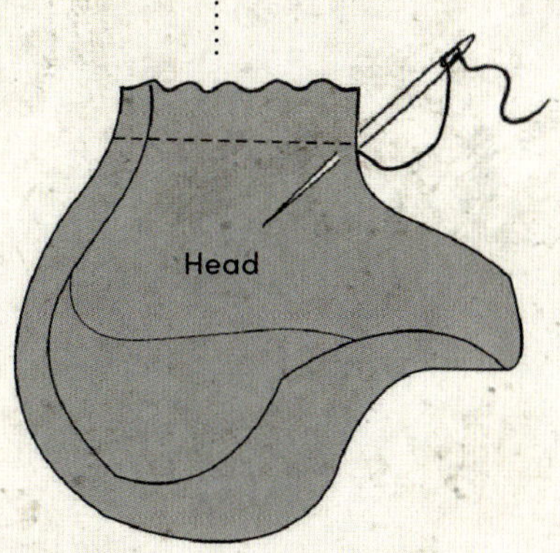

5

Now it's time to make the face. Using pins, place the bead eyes and nose on the face and move them around until you are happy with the position, then sew them on. Do the same thing with the ears, making sure the white felt faces forwards.

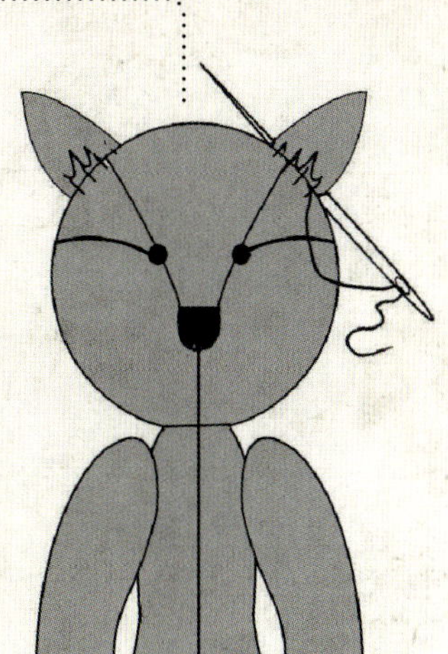

6

Using three strands of black embroidery thread (floss), back stitch the mouth. (Draw it on first with an erasable fabric marker pen.) For the whiskers, thread your needle with a long piece of brown thread and pull it backwards and forwards through the cheeks six to eight times, leaving a loop each time. Cut through the loops, then cut the whiskers to the desired length. Secure with a dab of glue where the whiskers meet the fabric.

Chester's Wardrobe

Harris
jacket
Classic
trousers

Sapphire's Wardrobe

Perfect
petal jacket
Apron dress
with appliqué

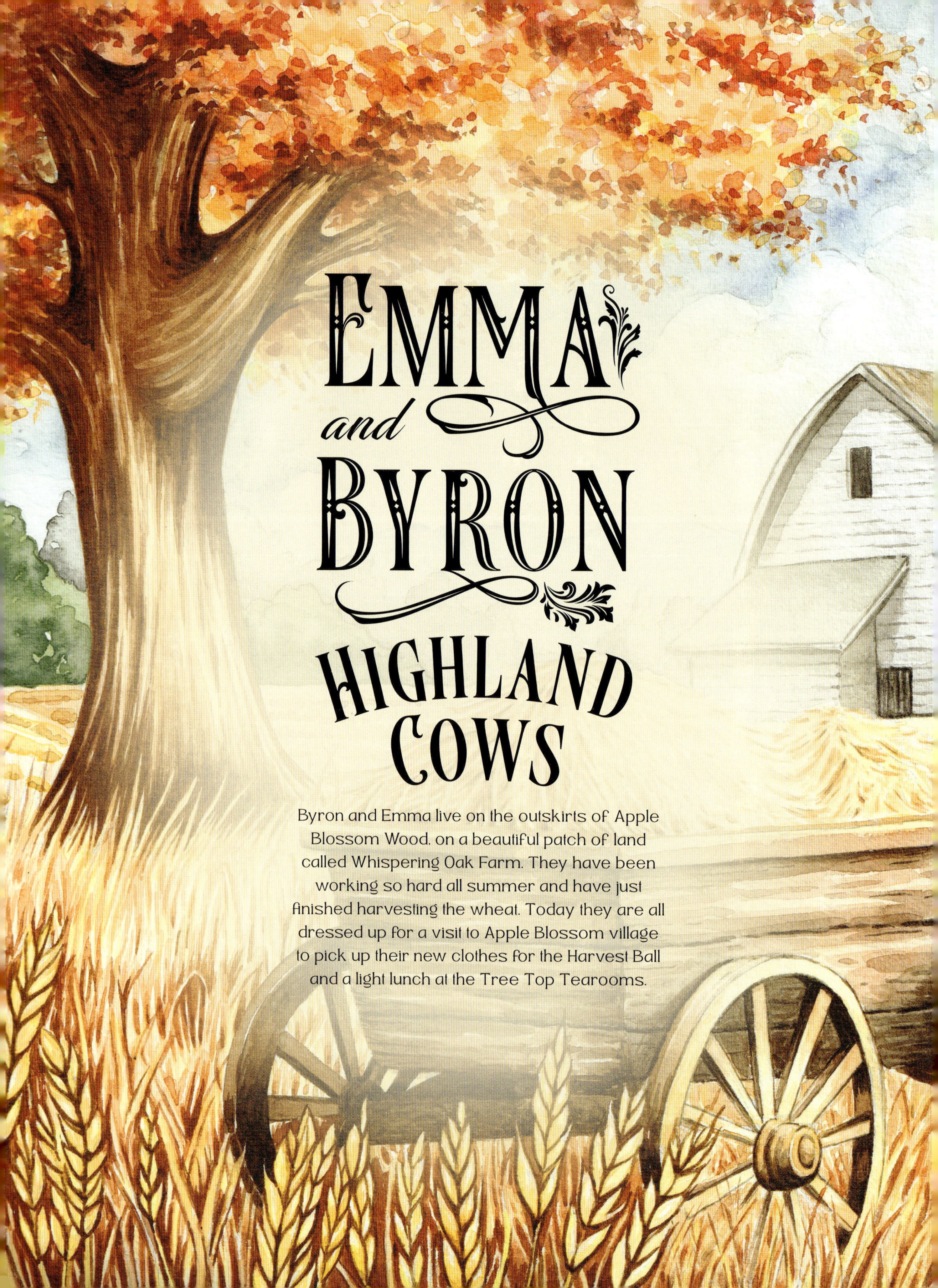

Emma and Byron Highland Cows

Byron and Emma live on the outskirts of Apple Blossom Wood, on a beautiful patch of land called Whispering Oak Farm. They have been working so hard all summer and have just finished harvesting the wheat. Today they are all dressed up for a visit to Apple Blossom village to pick up their new clothes for the Harvest Ball and a light lunch at the Tree Top Tearooms.

EMMA & BYRON

You will need

- Universal animal templates: Body, arm, leg
- Highland cow templates: Side head, head gusset, ear, tail, horn, head fur (front and back)
- 50 x 50cm (20 x 20in) marl terracotta wool felt for head, arms, body, legs and ears
- 26 x 10cm (10 x 4in) marl beige wool felt for horns
- 5 x 5cm (2 x 2in) cream wool felt for muzzle
- 25 x 50cm (10 x 20in) foxy deluxe 60mm (2½in) pile fur for head and tail fur
- 250g (8oz) toy filling
- 2 x 6mm (¼in) black beads for eyes
- Matching sewing thread
- Doll needle 15cm (6in)
- Dark grey craft chalk for nose
- 3 small craft paper roses for Emma

FINISHED SIZE: 40cm (16in)

All of the animals are made in the same way as Bertie Bear, with some modifications for the heads.

1

With right sides together, matching points A and B, pin the gusset to one head piece. Tack (baste) and sew along the drawn line. Attach the other side of the gusset to the other head piece in the same way. Trim the seam allowances.

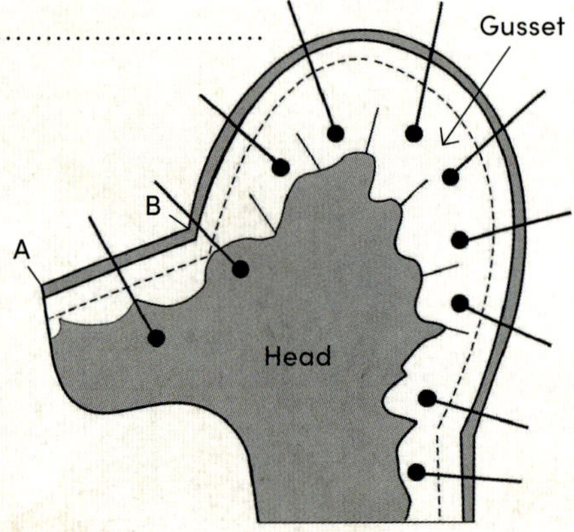

2

Following your drawn line, pin and sew from the nose (point A) to the neck, leaving the neck open. Trim the seam allowances.

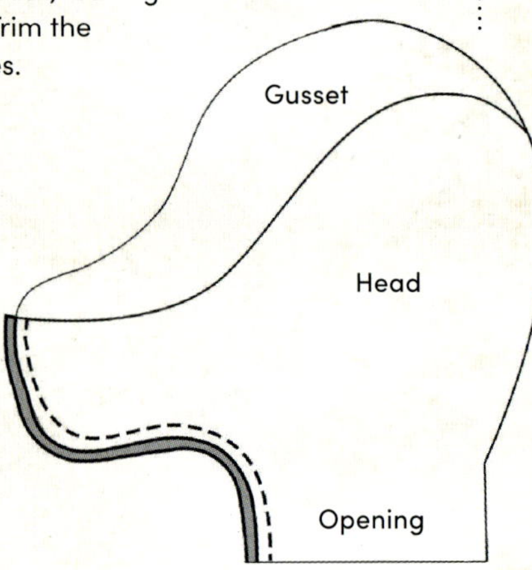

3

Turn the head right side out and fill with toy filling. Gather the neck edge of the head by hand, pull the threads tightly and oversew the edges of the neck together.

Make and assemble the body, arms, legs and ears, following the instructions for Bertie Bear, steps 3–9.

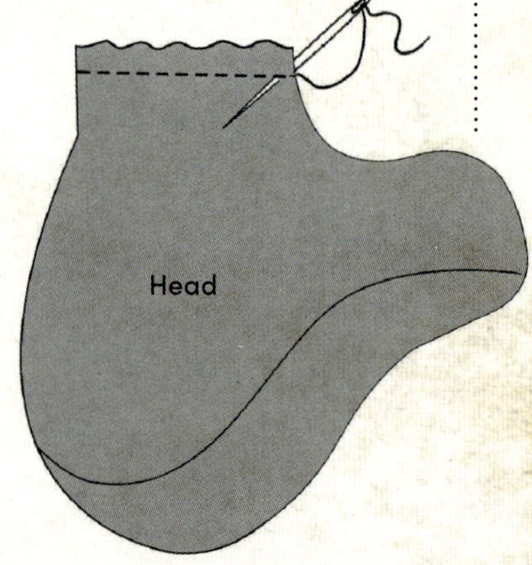

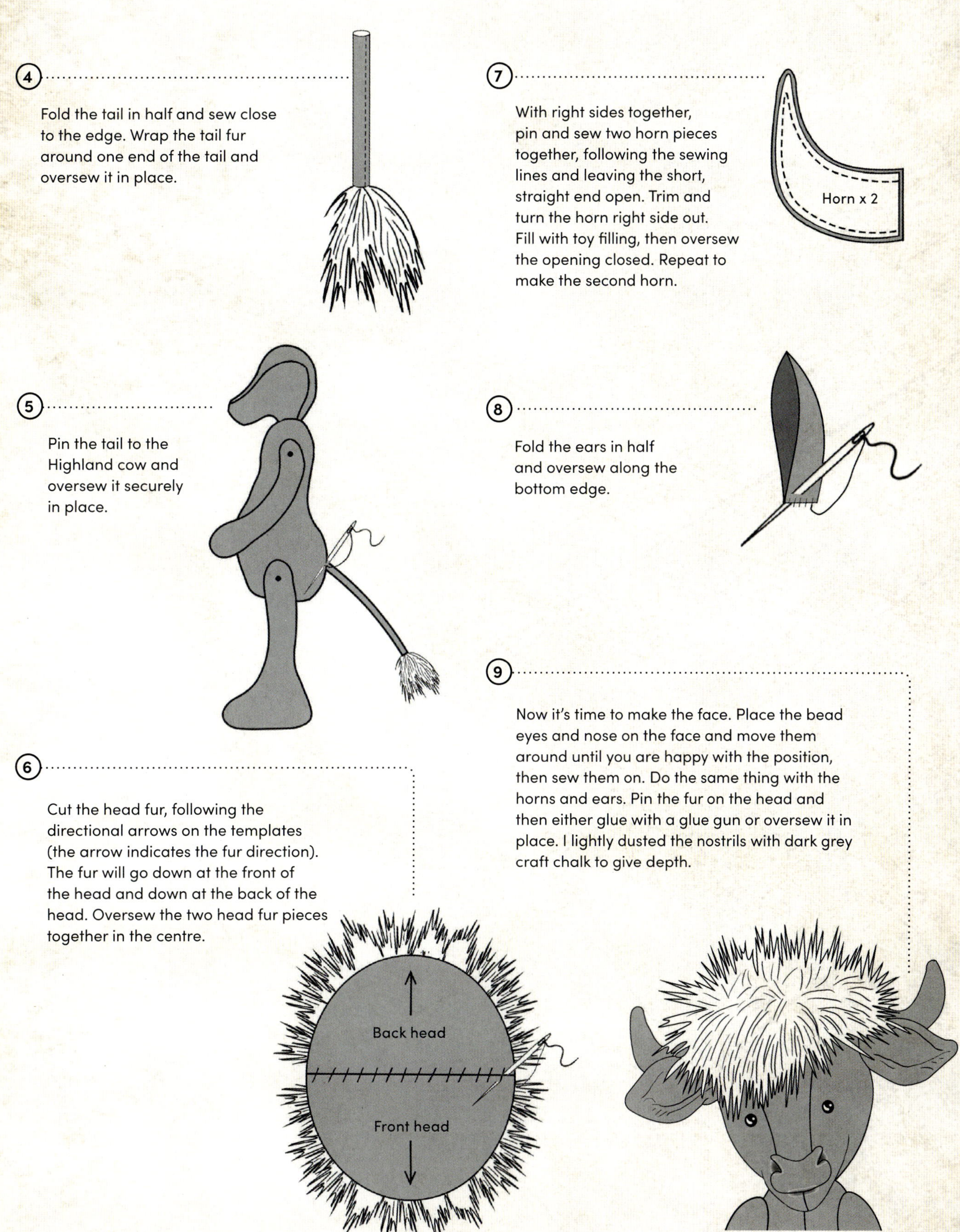

4

Fold the tail in half and sew close to the edge. Wrap the tail fur around one end of the tail and oversew it in place.

5

Pin the tail to the Highland cow and oversew it securely in place.

6

Cut the head fur, following the directional arrows on the templates (the arrow indicates the fur direction). The fur will go down at the front of the head and down at the back of the head. Oversew the two head fur pieces together in the centre.

7

With right sides together, pin and sew two horn pieces together, following the sewing lines and leaving the short, straight end open. Trim and turn the horn right side out. Fill with toy filling, then oversew the opening closed. Repeat to make the second horn.

8

Fold the ears in half and oversew along the bottom edge.

9

Now it's time to make the face. Place the bead eyes and nose on the face and move them around until you are happy with the position, then sew them on. Do the same thing with the horns and ears. Pin the fur on the head and then either glue with a glue gun or oversew it in place. I lightly dusted the nostrils with dark grey craft chalk to give depth.

Bella
bloomers
Josephine
jacket

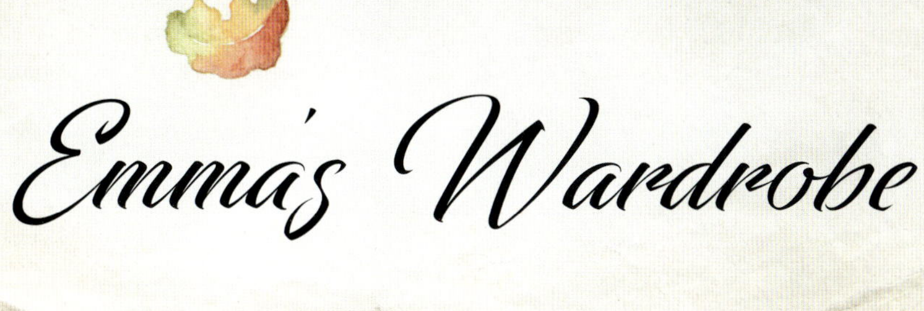

Apron
dress

Byron's Wardrobe

Regency jacket

Mandarin
waistcoat
Darcy
trousers

WARDROBE

In this section of the book, you will find all the instructions you need to make the animals' clothes. All the garments have been designed to look like authentic vintage attire, so there are apron dresses and frilly bloomers for the girls and snazzy waistcoats and classic trouser styles for the boys. I've given you a suggested wardrobe for each animal, but in fact all the clothes are interchangeable so you can mix and match to your heart's content – and, of course, you can embellish the garments in any way you choose, with pretty patch pockets, simple appliqué motifs or beautiful embroidery.

Remember

Use lightweight fabrics, as they will be easier to work with, especially when turning out, and choose small-patterned fabric that will be in scale with the animals. It's also important to trim and neaten seam allowances and press at every stage of the construction process.

Austen Waistcoat

You will need

- Templates: Front, back
- 17 x 56cm (6½ x 22in) cotton fabric
- 17 x 56cm (6½ x 22in) cotton fabric for lining
- Matching sewing thread
- 8 x 7mm (¼in) buttons
- 3 x 7mm (¼in) snap fasteners

1. To make the back darts, fold the fabric right sides together between the dots marked on the template and sew in place. With right sides together, pin and sew the waistcoat front to the waistcoat back at the side seams and press the seams open. Trim the seam allowances. Repeat for the waistcoat lining.

2. With right sides together, sew the waistcoat to the waistcoat lining, leaving an opening at the bottom of the centre back. Clip the corners and trim the seam allowances. Turn the waistcoat right side out.

3. Oversew the shoulder seams together, then oversew the opening at the centre back to close it.

4. Add eight buttons to the left front of the waistcoat. Overlap the left front on the right front and sew three snap fasteners behind the buttons to secure.

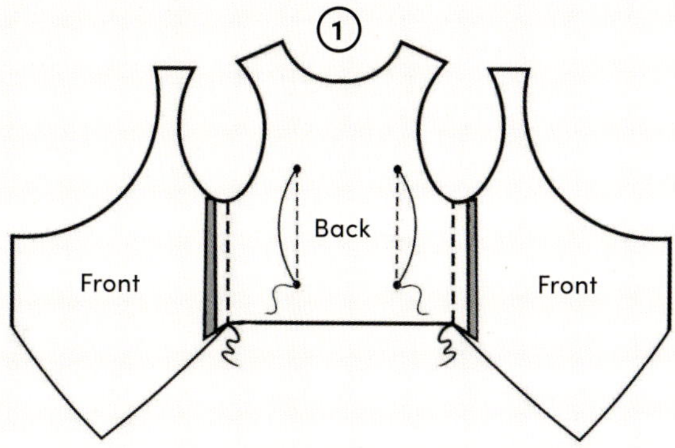

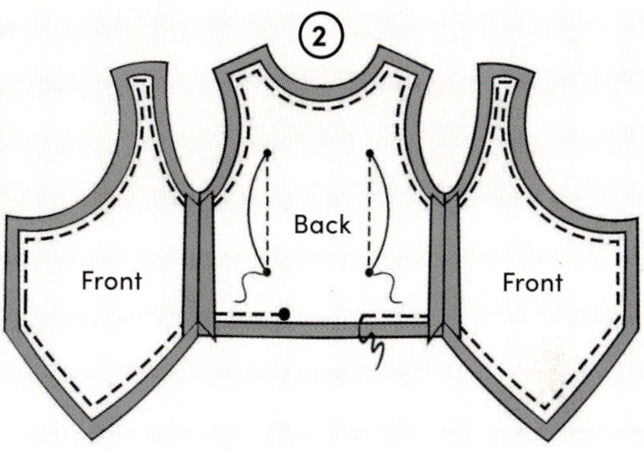

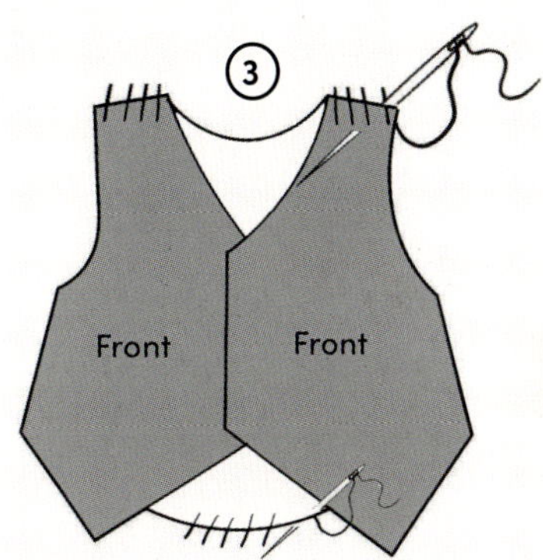

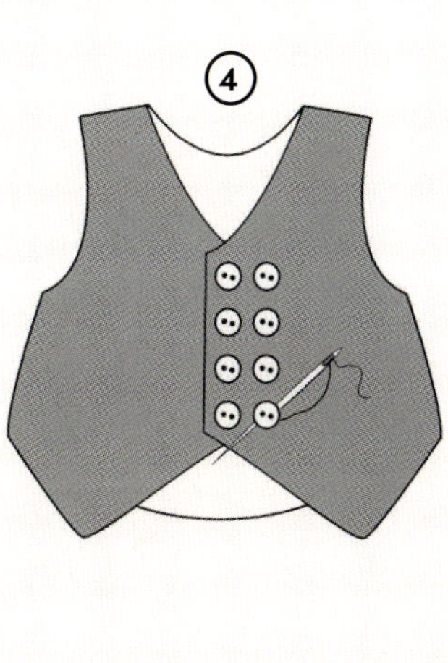

Classic Shirt

You will need

- Templates: Front, back, back facing, sleeve, collar
- 20 x 115cm (8 x 44in) cotton fabric
- Matching sewing thread
- 5 x 4mm (⅛in) buttons
- 4 x 7mm (¼in) snap fasteners

1. With right sides together, sew the collar pieces together along the short side edges and the outer curved edge. Trim the seam allowances, turn right side out and press.

2. Neaten the edges of the shirt fronts and the curved outer edge of the back facing by oversewing or with zigzag stitch.

3. Sew the shirt fronts to the shirt back at the shoulder seams and neaten the edges by oversewing or with zigzag stitch.

4. With right sides together, tack (baste) the collar in place.

5. Sew the back facing to the front facings at the shoulder seams from A to A, then fold the front facings down the line marked on the template and press. Sew around the neckline, trim the seam allowances and turn the front facings to the wrong side of the garment.

6. Fold the bottom edge of the sleeves up twice by 3mm (⅛in) and sew in place. Around the sleeve heads, sew two rows of gather stitch inside the seam allowances between the points marked on the template.

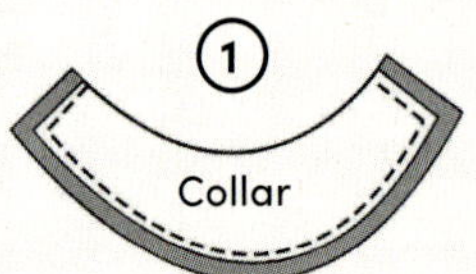

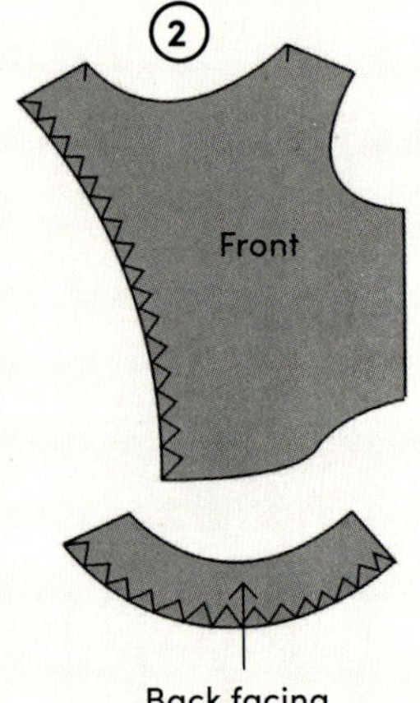

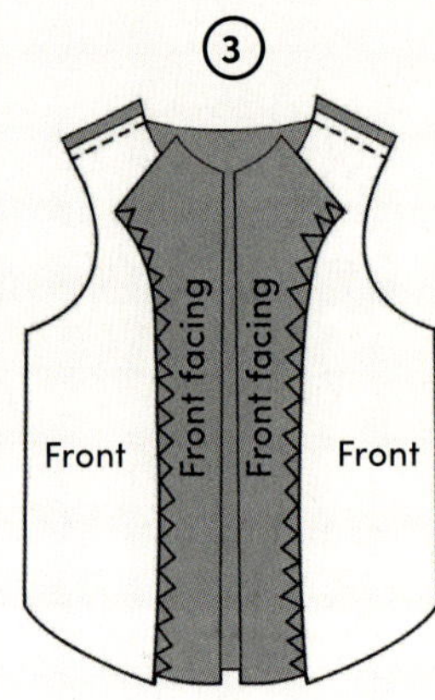

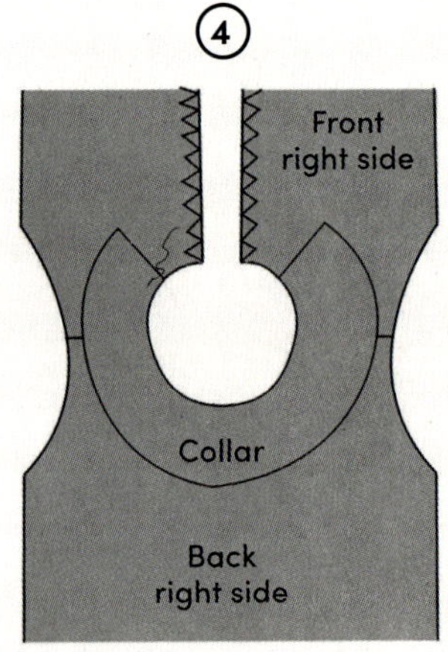

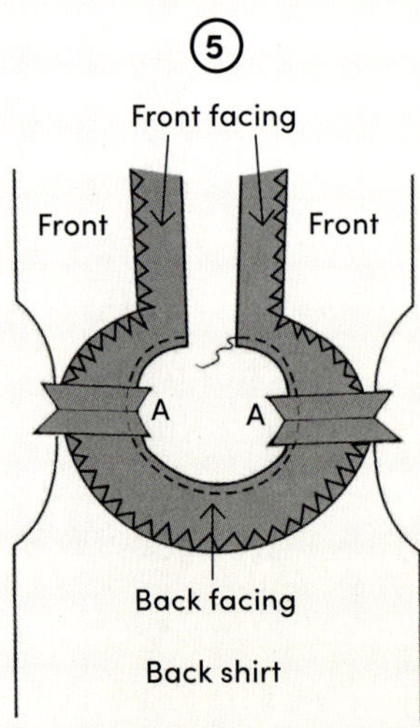

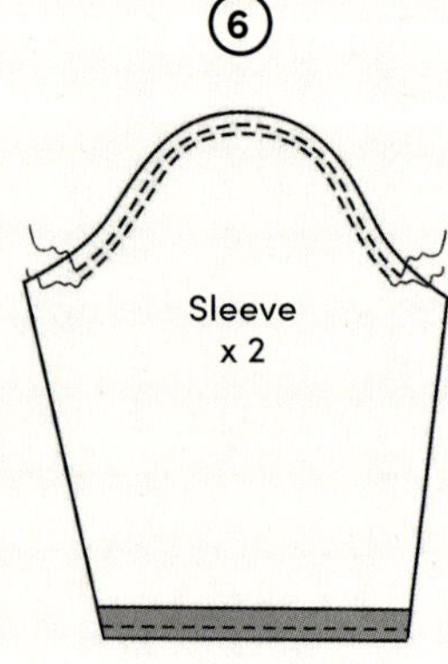

7. With right sides down, pin the sleeves to the armholes. Pull up the gather stitches gently to fit, then tack (baste) and sew in place. Neaten the seam allowances.

8. With right sides together, sew the underarm and side seams. Trim and neaten the edges. Fold the bottom edge of the shirt up twice by 3mm (⅛in) and sew in place.

9. Add five buttons to the left front of the shirt. Overlap the left front on the right front and sew four snap fasteners behind the buttons to secure.

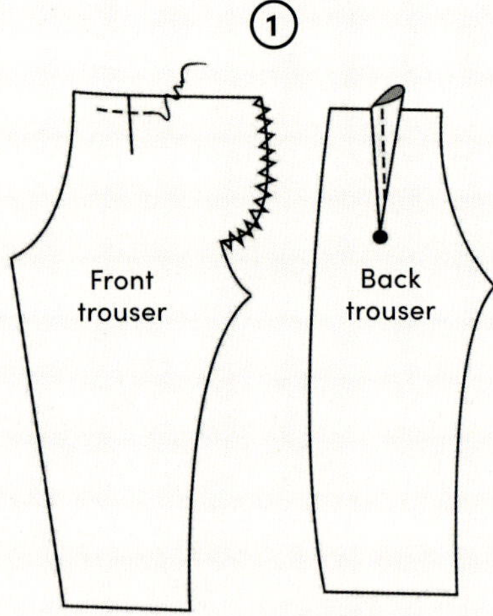

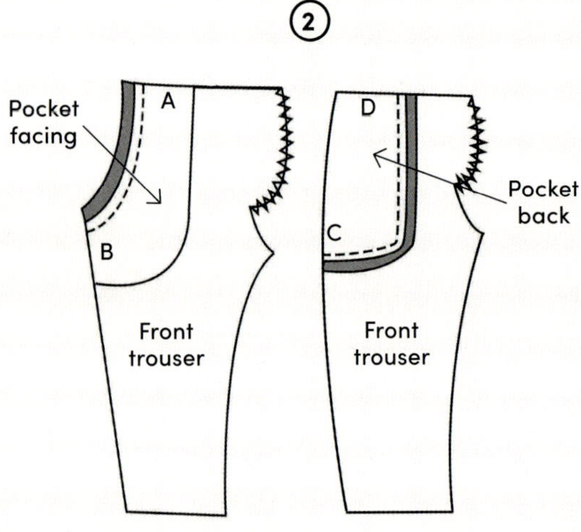

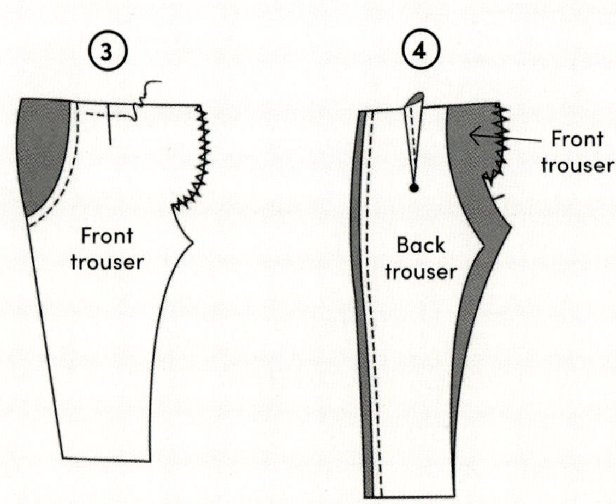

Classic Trousers

You will need

- Templates: Front leg, back leg, waistband, pocket facing, pocket back
- 40 x 56cm (16 x 22in) cotton flannel
- Matching sewing thread
- 1 x 4mm (⅛in) button
- 1 x 7mm (¼in) snap fastener

1. Pin and tack (baste) a pleat in the waistline of each front trouser leg, following the markings on the template. Neaten the trouser openings on the front legs. Pin and sew a waist dart in each back trouser leg.

2. With right sides together, sew a pocket facing to the right side of each front trouser leg between A and B. With right sides together, sew a pocket back to each pocket facing from C to D, then neaten the edge.

3. Trim the seam between A and B. Turn the pocket and its facing over to the wrong side of the trouser leg. Topstitch, remembering to leave the back part of the pocket free.

4. Sew a back and a front trouser leg together at the side seam and neaten the edge. Repeat with the second front and back trouser legs. Press the seams open.

5. Hem the bottom edge of each trouser leg by turning up 6mm (¼in) twice, and sewing in place.

6. Sew the centre front and centre back seams and neaten the edges.

7. Bring the centre seams together and sew the inside leg seams. Trim and neaten the edges.

8. With wrong sides together, press the waistband in half widthways. Pin the waistband around the top of the trousers, right sides together, and sew in place around the top edge. (The waistband will extend beyond the trousers on one side of the front to allow room to attach a snap fastener.) Press the waistband up, away from the trousers.

9. Fold the waistband along the crease made in step 8. Fold the raw edge of the waistband under and press, making sure the waistband is a consistent width all the way around. Oversew in place. Add a button and snap fastener to the front of the trousers to secure.

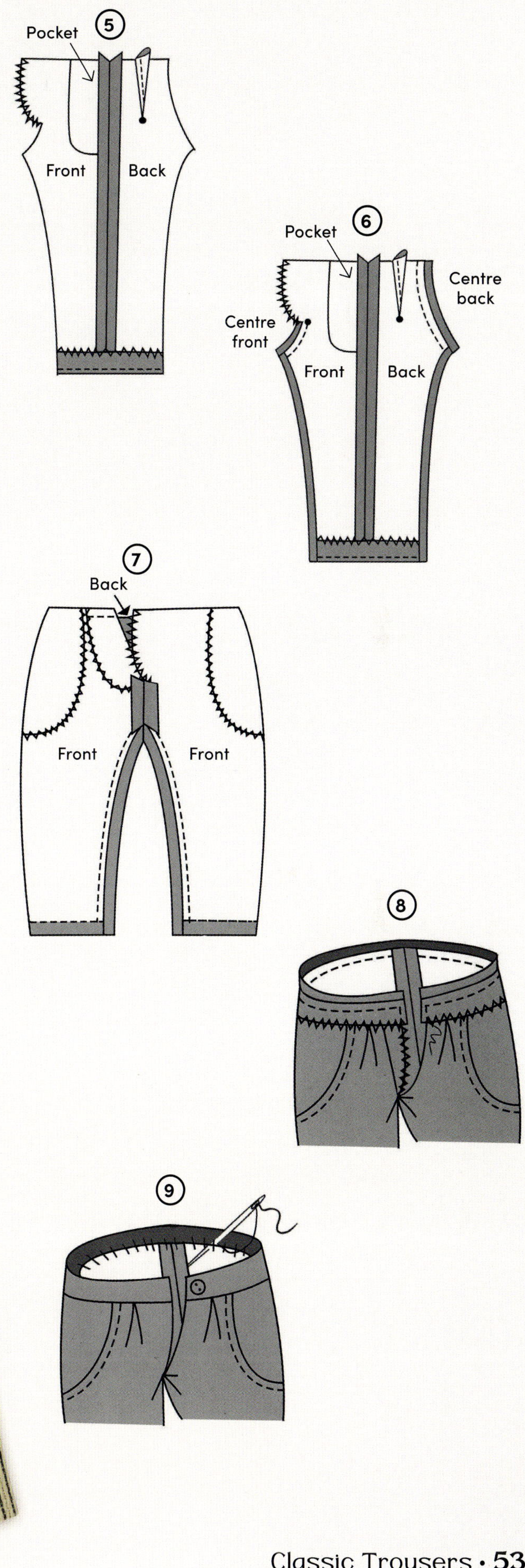

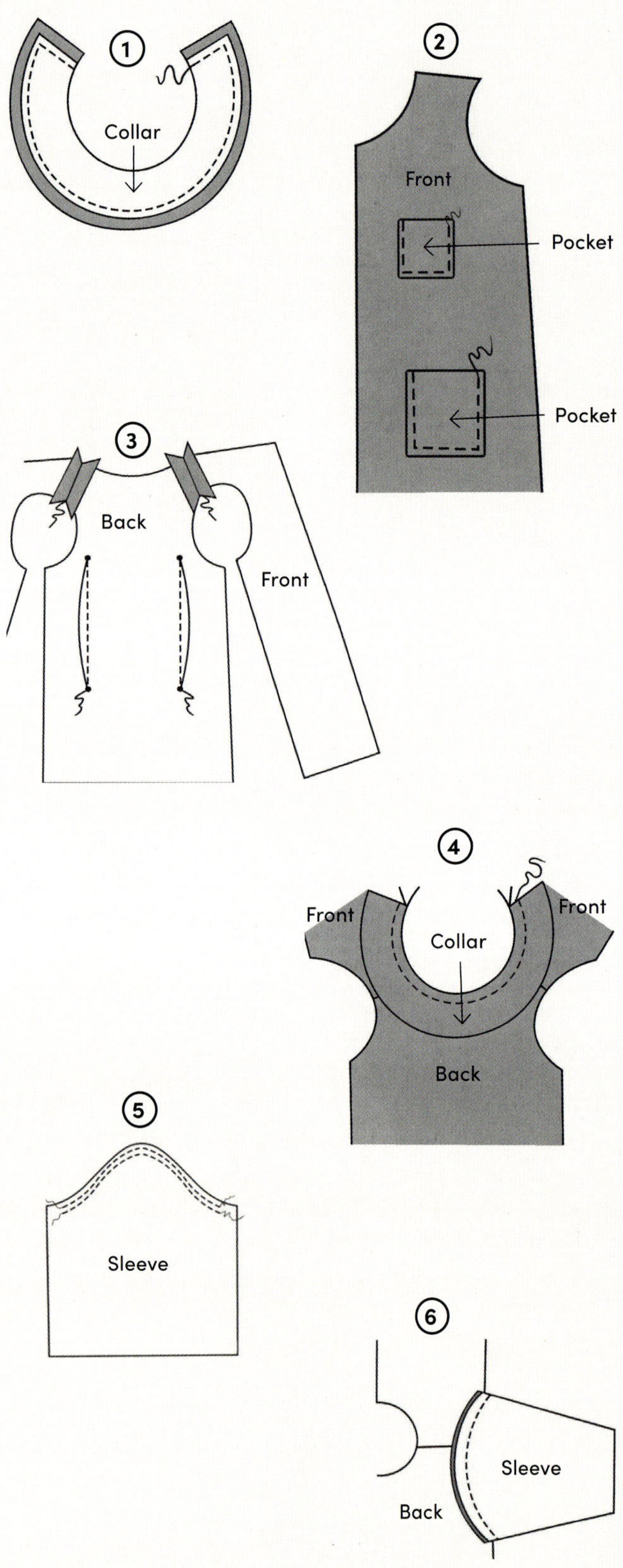

Shelby Coat

You will need

- Templates: Front, back, sleeve, sleeve lining, collar, pockets
- 30 x 115cm (12 x 44in) cotton flannel
- 30 x 56cm (12 x 22in) cotton cotton fabric for lining
- Matching sewing thread

1. With right sides together, sew the collar pieces together along the short side edges and the outer curved edge. Trim the seam allowances, turn right side out and press.

2. To make the pockets, fold and press all four edges to the wrong side by 6mm (¼in). Position the pockets on the coat fronts, using the guide on the template. Topstitch in place around the side and bottom edges.

3. To make the back darts, fold the fabric right sides together between the dots marked on the template, pin and sew in place. With right sides together, join the fronts to the back at the shoulder seams. Repeat for the lining. Trim the seam allowances and press the seams open.

4. Place the collar on the right side of the coat, matching A to A. Tack (baste) in place.

5. Around the sleeve head, sew two rows of gather stitch inside the seam allowance between the points marked on the template.

6. With right sides down, pin the sleeve to the armhole edge. Pull up the gather stitches gently to fit. Tack (baste) and then sew in place. Repeat for other sleeve and the coat lining. Trim the seam allowances.

7. Sew the underarm and side seams of the coat in one continuous line of stitching. Trim the seam allowances.

8. Repeat with the lining, leaving an opening on one side so that the coat can be pulled through. Trim the seam allowances.

9. With right sides together, pin and tack (baste) the coat and lining together, sandwiching the collar in between. Sew all around, trim and turn out through the side opening in the lining. Oversew the lining opening closed.

10. To neaten the sleeves, fold the sleeves and sleeve lining back to the right side. Turn the sleeve lining under by 6mm (¼in) and oversew it to the sleeve.

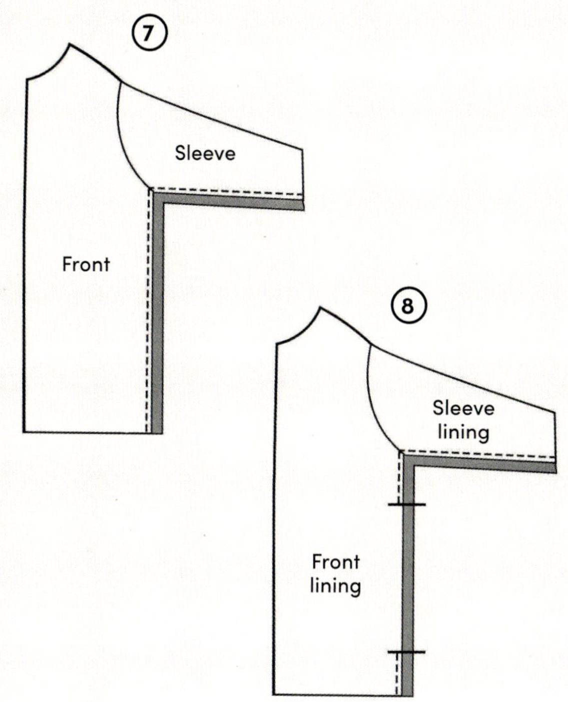

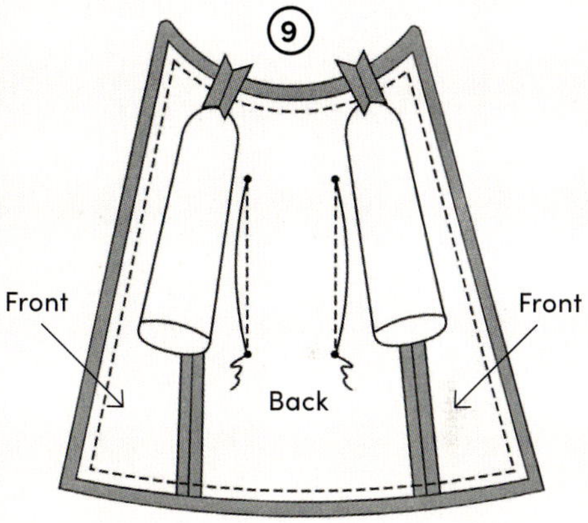

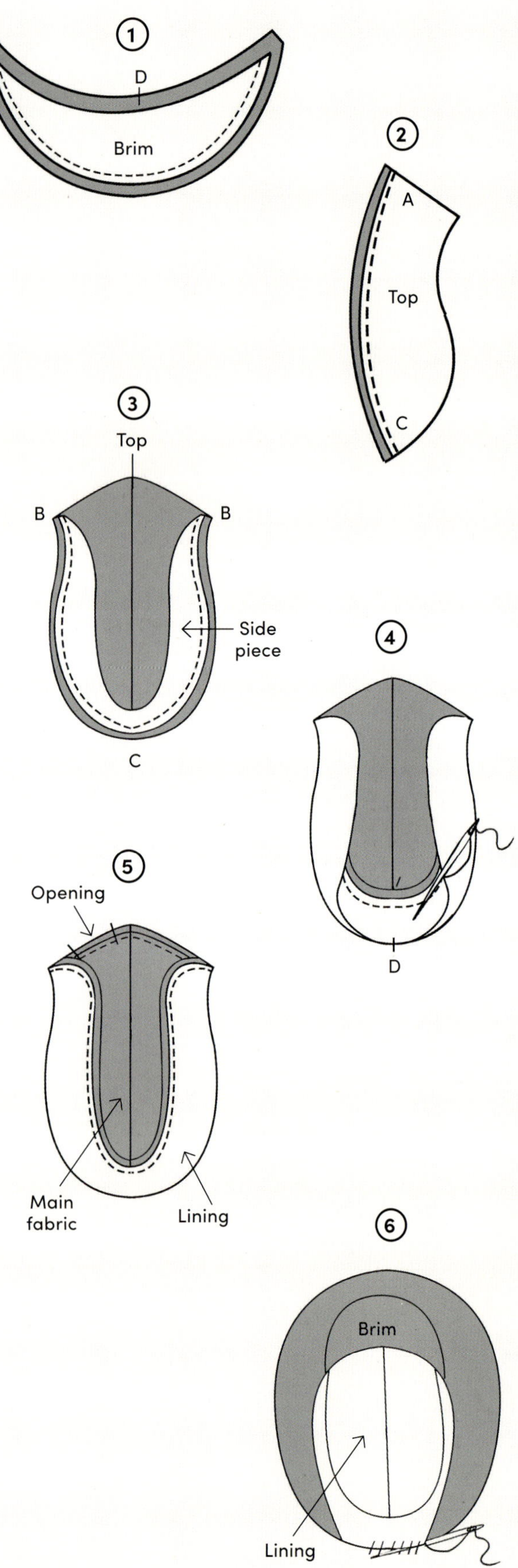

PEAKY CAP

You will need

- Templates: Brim, top, side
- 30 x 56cm (12 x 22in) cotton flannel or woven fabric
- 30 x 56cm (12 x 22in) cotton fabric for lining
- Small amount of iron-on interfacing
- Matching sewing thread

1. Apply iron-on interfacing to the wrong side of one brim piece. With right sides together, sew the brim pieces together along the curved outer edge. Trim, turn right side out and press.

2. With right sides together, sew the two main fabric top cap pieces together between A and C. Repeat with the lining top cap pieces. Open out and press the seam allowances open.

3. With right sides together, pin the main fabric side piece to the main fabric top cap piece from B to C and back to B, along the curved outer edge. You will have to tease the fabric round the curve to fit. Tack (baste) in place and sew. Repeat with the lining top and side pieces. Trim.

4. Tack (baste) the brim to the underside of the cap, making sure the centres match at D.

5. With right sides together, sew the cap and lining together, leaving a gap so that it can be turned right side out.

6. Trim and turn the cap right side out, then oversew the opening closed.

Horseshoe Waistcoat

You will need

- Templates: Front, back, collar, pocket
- 15 x 56cm (6 x 22in) lightweight woven fabric
- 15 x 56cm (6 x 22in) cotton fabric for lining
- Matching sewing thread
- Contrasting stranded embroidery thread (floss)
- 4 x 5mm (3⁄16in) brass buttons
- 4 x 5mm (3⁄16in) snap fasteners

1. With right sides together, sew two collar pieces together along the short curved side and one long side. Trim and turn right side out. Repeat with the remaining two collar pieces.

2. With right sides together, tack (baste) the collars to the right side of the waistcoat fronts.

3. With right sides together, sew two pocket pieces together, leaving an opening in one long side. Trim, turn right side out and oversew the opening closed. Repeat with the remaining two pocket pieces.

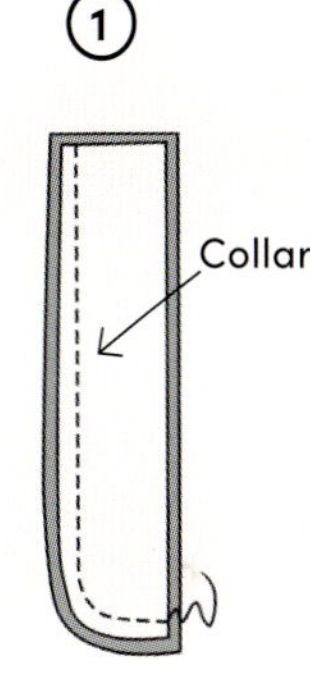

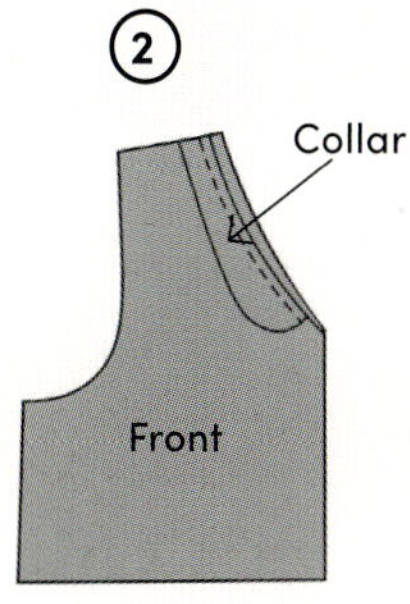

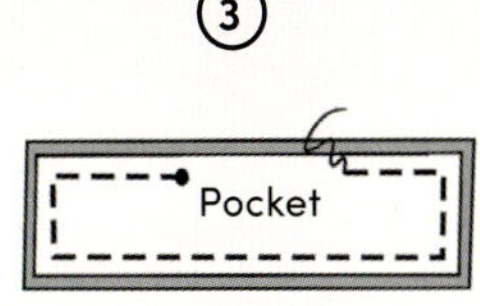

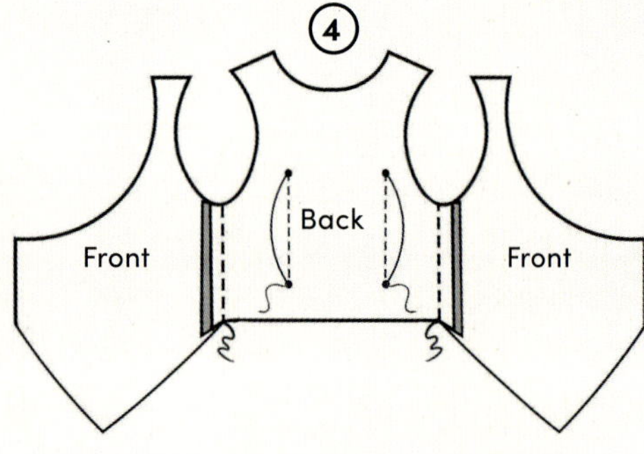

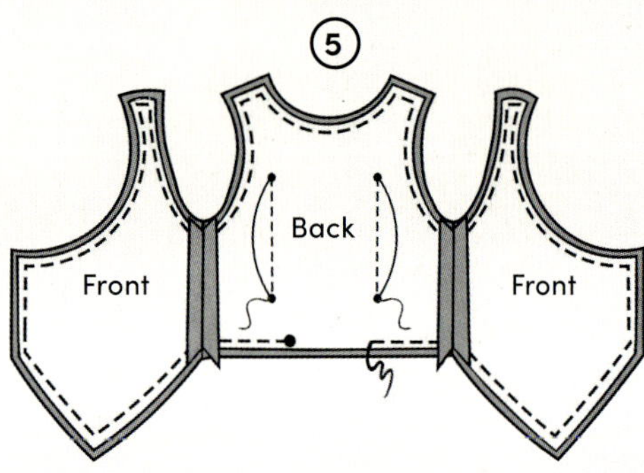

4. To make the back darts, fold the fabric right sides together between the dots marked on the template, pin and sew in place. Pin and sew the waistcoat fronts to the waistcoat back at the side seams and press the seams open. Repeat with the waistcoat lining pieces.

5. With right sides together, sew the outer waistcoat to the waistcoat lining, leaving an opening at the bottom of the centre back. Clip the corners, trim and turn right side out.

6. Oversew the shoulder seams together and oversew the opening at the back closed.

7. Pin the pockets to the waistcoat fronts and oversew them in place. Overlap the left front on the right and sew four buttons to the left front. Add snap fasteners behind the buttons to secure. You can now add some detail by oversewing random stitches around the collar or pocket edges using three strands of embroidery thread (floss).

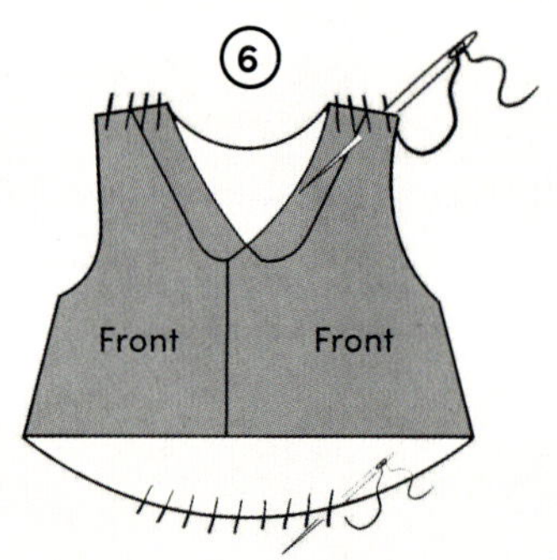

Swallowtail Jacket

You will need

- Templates: Front, back, sleeve, sleeve lining, collar
- 40 x 56cm (16 x 22in) lightweight woven fabric
- 40 x 56cm (16 x 22in) cotton fabric for lining
- 2 x patches in contrast fabric, 5 x 8cm (2 x 3in)
- Matching sewing thread
- Contrasting stranded embroidery thread (floss)

1. With right sides together, pin and sew the two collar pieces together around the short sides and the curved outer edge. Clip the corners and trim the seam allowances. Turn right side out.

2. To make the back darts, fold the fabric right sides together between the dots marked on the template, pin and sew in place. With right sides together, pin and sew the fronts to the back at the shoulders. Trim the seam allowances and press the seams open. Repeat for the lining.

3. Tack (baste) the collar to the right side of the jacket between the marked As.

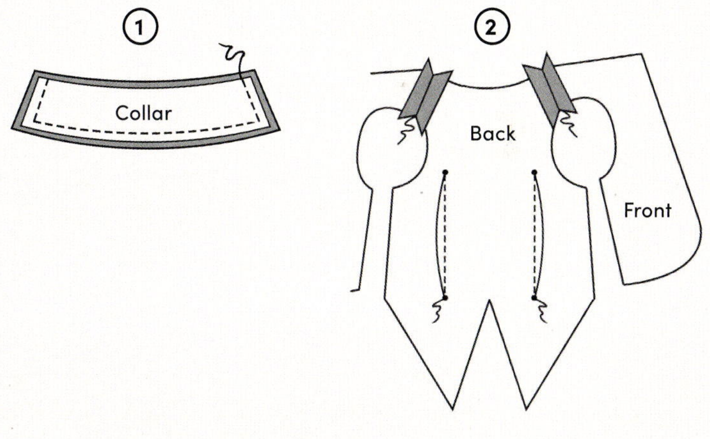

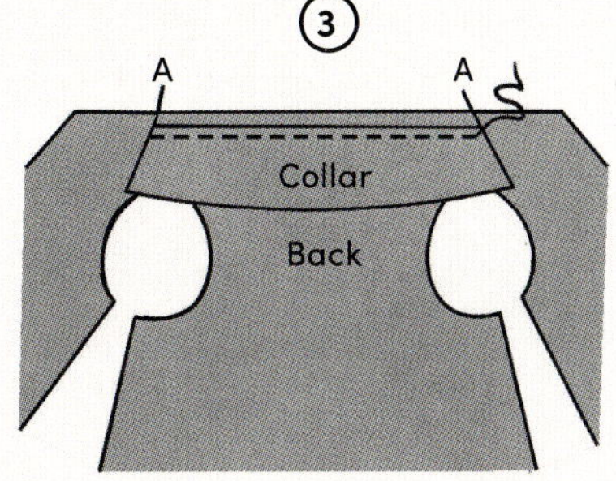

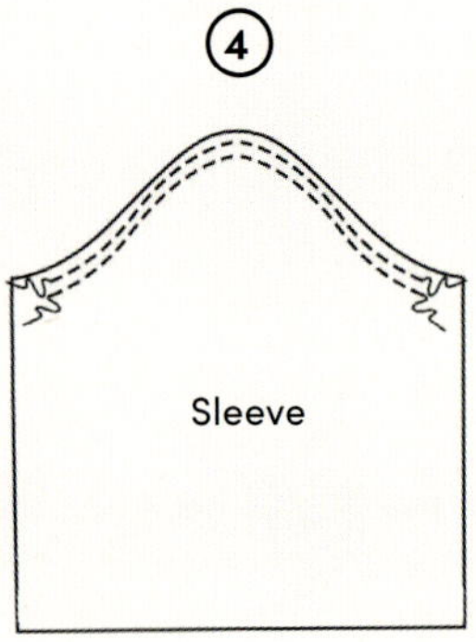

4

Sleeve

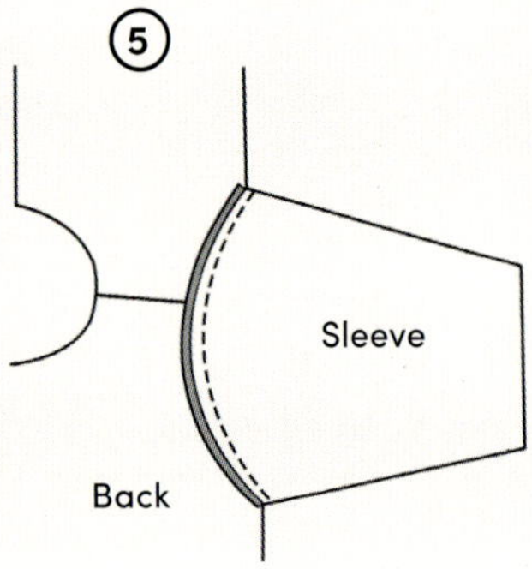

5

Sleeve

Back

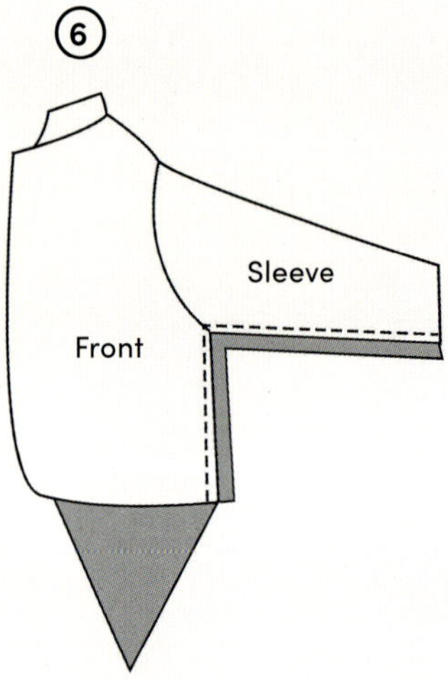

6

Sleeve

Front

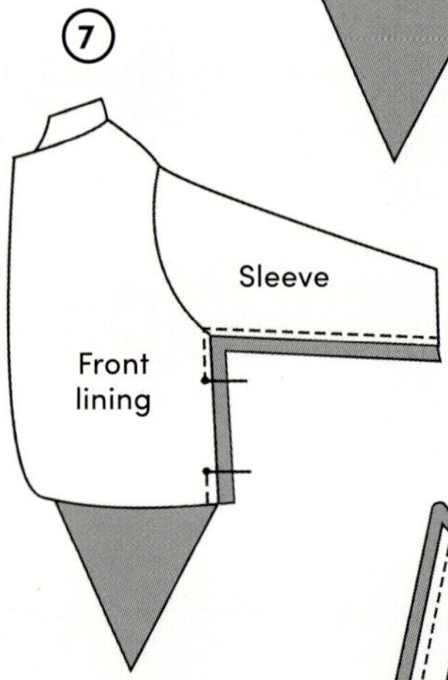

7

Sleeve

Front lining

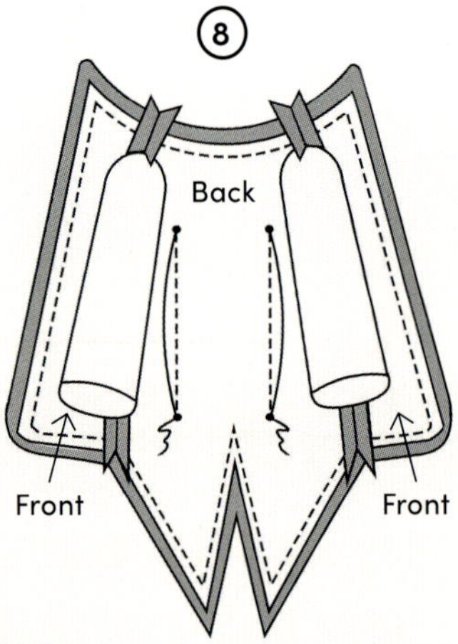

8

Back

Front

Front

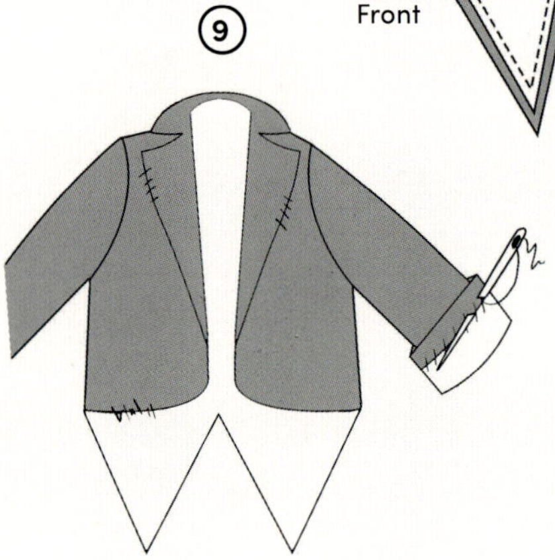

9

4. Around the sleeve head, sew two rows of gather stitch inside the seam allowance between the points marked on the template.

5. With right sides down, pin the sleeve to the armhole. Pull up the gather stitches gently to fit, then tack (baste) and sew in place. Repeat for the other sleeve and the jacket lining. Trim the seam allowances.

6. With right sides together, pin and sew the underarm and side seams of the jacket in one continuous line of stitching on each side. Trim the seam allowances.

7. Repeat with the lining, leaving an opening on one side so that the jacket can be pulled through. Trim the seam allowances.

8. With right sides together, pin and tack (baste) the jacket and lining together. Sew round, trim and turn out through the side opening in the lining. Oversew the lining opening closed.

9. To neaten the sleeves, fold the sleeves and sleeve lining back to the right side. Turn the sleeve lining under by 6mm (¼in) and oversew it to the sleeve. For Eli, sew some random stitches around the collar using three strands of embroidery thread (floss) and add small, frayed patches of contrast fabric to give the jacket a well-worn look.

Apron Dress

You will need

- Templates: Front bodice, back bodice, pocket; acorn appliqué motif for Sapphire only
- 22 x 115cm (8½ x 44in) cotton fabric
- Matching sewing thread
- 3 x 6mm (¼in) buttons
- 3 x 6mm (¼in) snap fasteners

For the appliqué variation only:

- 10 x 10cm (4 x 4in) cotton fabric in each of 2 shades of brown for appliqué acorns
- 10 x 10cm (4 x 4in) green cotton fabric for appliqué leaves
- Contrasting sewing thread (or stranded embroidery thread/floss) if appliquéing by hand
- 20 x 30cm (8 x 12in) fusible bonding web

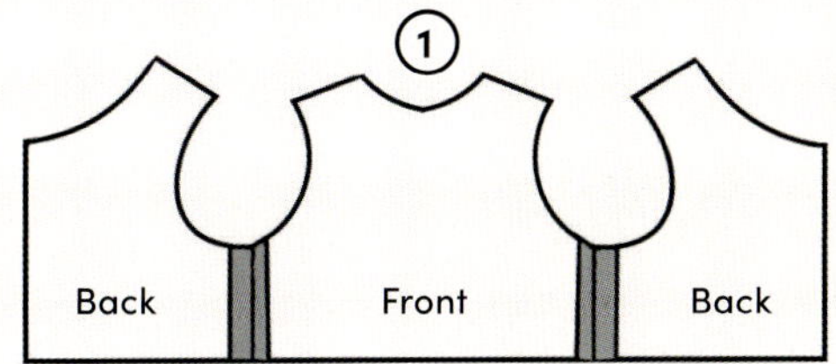

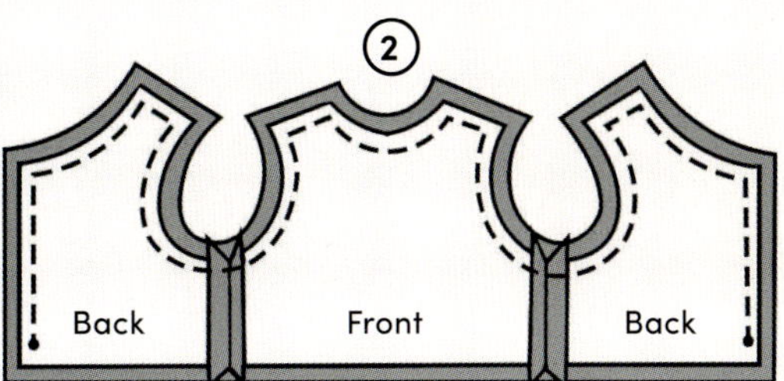

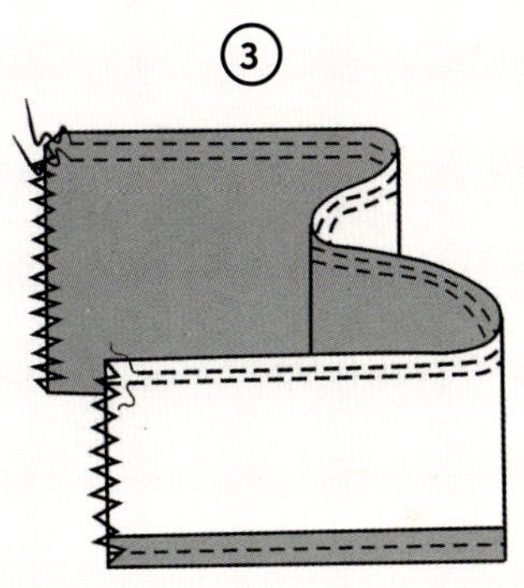

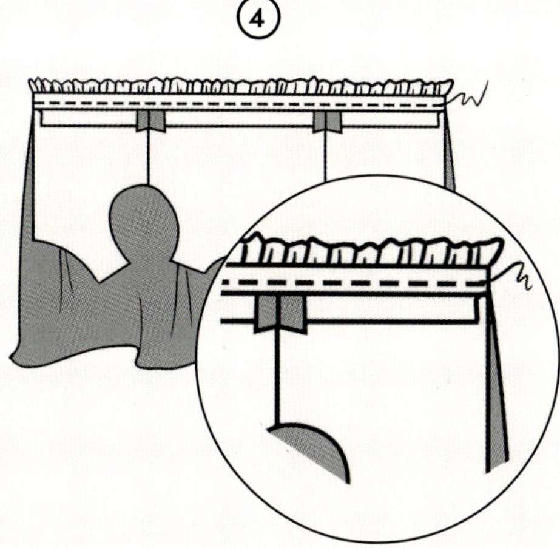

1. With right sides together, pin and sew the bodice back pieces to the bodice front at the side seams. Trim the seam allowances and press the seams open. Repeat for the bodice lining pieces

2. With right sides together, pin and sew the bodice to the bodice lining, leaving the bottom edge open. Snip the corners and trim the seam allowances. Turn right side out.

3. To make the skirt, cut a piece of fabric measuring 82 x 22cm (33 x 8½in). Neaten the side and bottom edges. (Elisha has a frayed edge to her skirt, so you can miss neatening if you wish.) To gather the top of the skirt, sew two rows of running stitch inside the seam allowance.

4. Gather the skirt to fit the bottom edge of the outer bodice and pin them right sides together. Sew in place, taking care not to sew through the lining bodice.

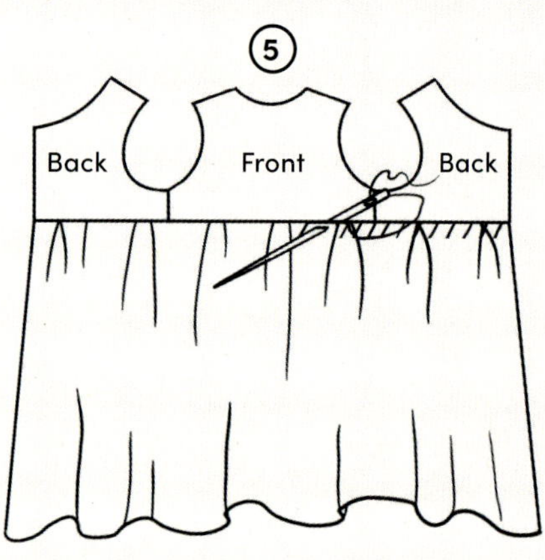

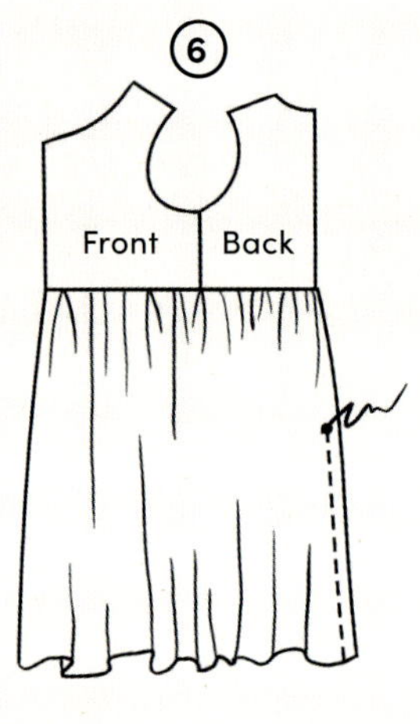

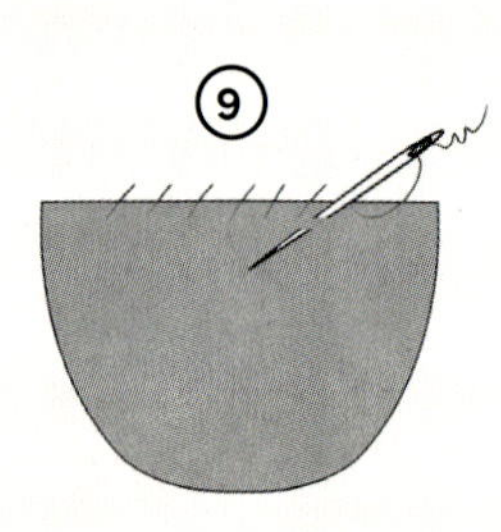

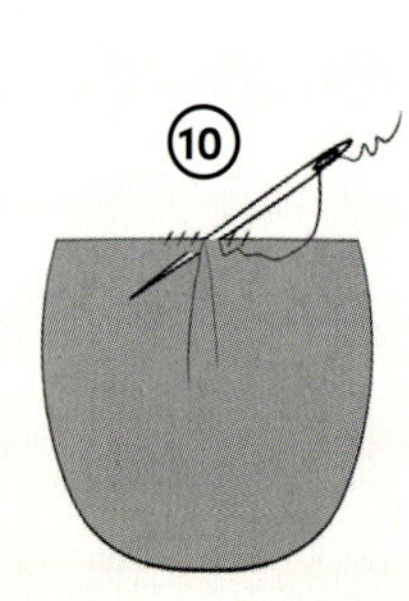

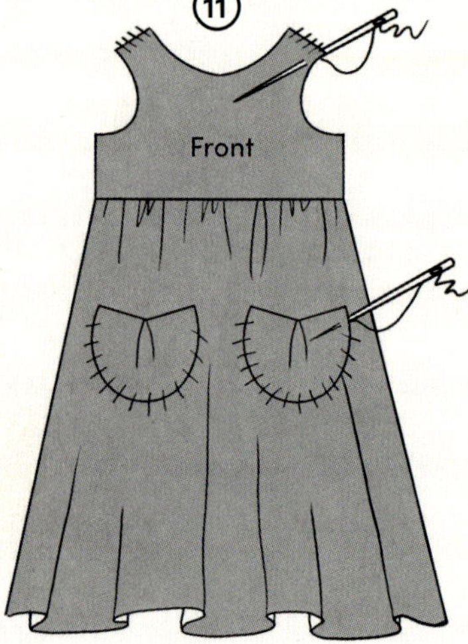

5. Trim the outer bodice and skirt seam allowances and press them up, towards the bodice. Fold the bottom edge of the lining bodice over them, then oversew it to the bottom edge of the bodice .

6. With right sides together, sew the skirt together at the back seam, leaving an opening of 7.5cm (3in) at the top of the skirt for the tail to fit through. Trim and neaten the opening by making a double 3mm (⅛in) fold and sewing it in place.

7. To fasten the dress, overlap the left back bodice over the right and sew on three snap fasteners, then sew three small buttons on the right side of the back opening.

8. With right sides together, sew two pocket pieces together, leaving an opening at the top. Trim and turn right side out. Repeat with the remaining two pocket pieces.

9. Oversew the opening closed.

10. Fold the pocket at the centre, as indicated on the template, and oversew.

11. To finish the apron dress, oversew the shoulder seams together. Place the pockets on the skirt. When you are happy with their position, oversew them on. Elisha has random stitches on her dress, using three strands of embroidery thread (floss). To finish your dress you can cut small squares of fabric that you can fray and sew onto the dress using blanket stitch to create a worn look.

APPLIQUÉ VARIATION

This variation is for Sapphire's Apron Dress. Work the appliqué on the skirt once you've neatened the side and bottom edges, before you sew the gather stitches.

1. Trace the template for the acorns onto the wrong side (not the glue side) of the fusible bonding web, leaving a good-sized gap between acorn and shell. Repeat for the leaves.

2. Apply the acorn, shells and leaves to the wrong side of your chosen fabrics, with a medium heat.

3. Cut around the templates and remove the paper backing.

4. Fold your skirt fabric in half to find the centre. Referring to the template, arrange the acorns, shells and leaves. Using a medium heat on your iron, press in place.

5. To neaten and secure, blanket stitch around the edge of each leaf and acorn by hand (using three strands of embroidery thread/floss) or by machine.

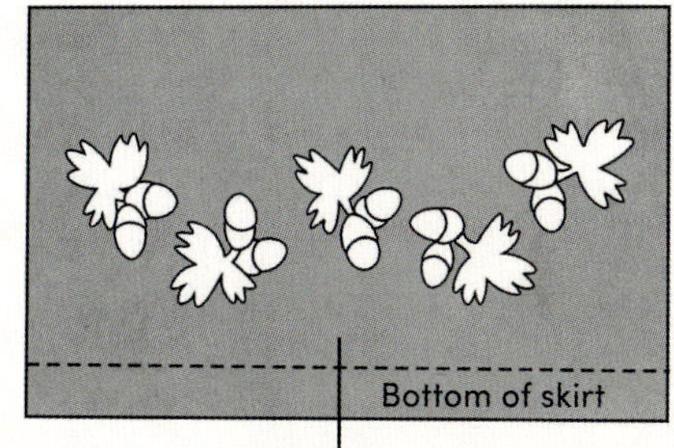

BELLA BLOOMERS

You will need

- Template: Leg
- 24 x 66cm (9¼ x 26in) cotton fabric
- 65cm (26in) lace, 6mm (¼in) wide
- 50cm (20in) elastic, 6mm (¼in) wide
- Matching sewing thread

For the ribbon bow variation only:

- 1m (39in) crushed ribbon, 6mm (¼in) wide

1. Neaten the raw edge at the bottom of the bloomer legs, then turn 6mm (¼in) to the wrong side. Pin the lace to the bottom of the legs on the wrong side and sew on.

2. Set your machine to a long, wide zigzag stitch and stitch across both bloomer legs 2cm (¾in) from the top of the lace; this will create a casing for the elastic. With right sides together, sew both legs together from the crotch to the top of the waist. Trim and neaten.

3. Fold each leg in half from the bottom of the crotch to the hem, right sides together. Sew from the bottom of the first leg to the crotch and back down the second leg. Trim and neaten.

4. Turn the waist edge over twice by 1cm (⅜in) to create a casing. Sew close to the bottom fold, leaving a small gap to thread the elastic. Thread elastic through the casing, making sure there is enough give to fit over the animal, then overlap the ends of the elastic, cut to the required length and stitch the ends together. Oversew the opening closed.

1

Bloomers

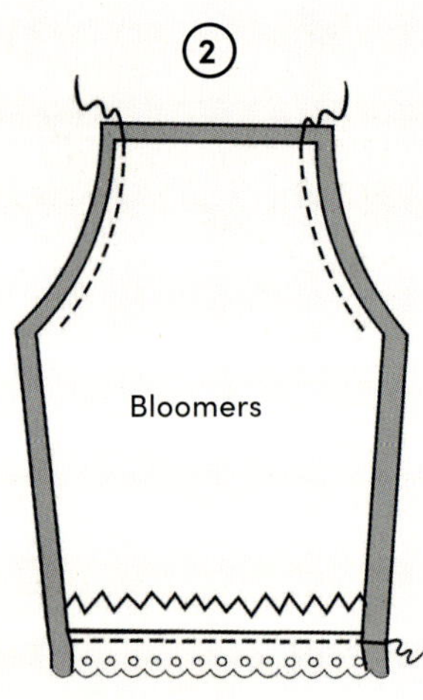

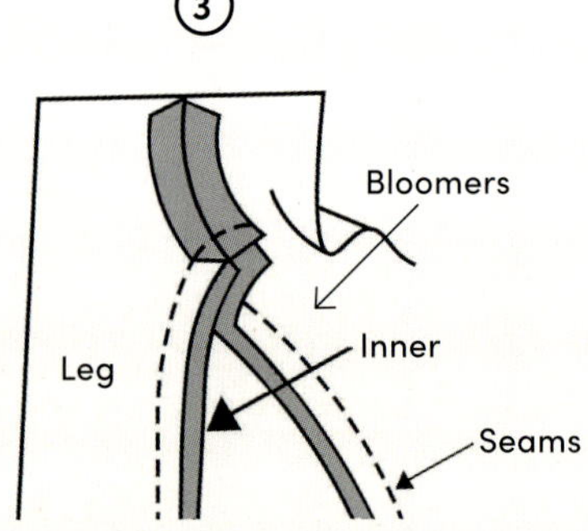

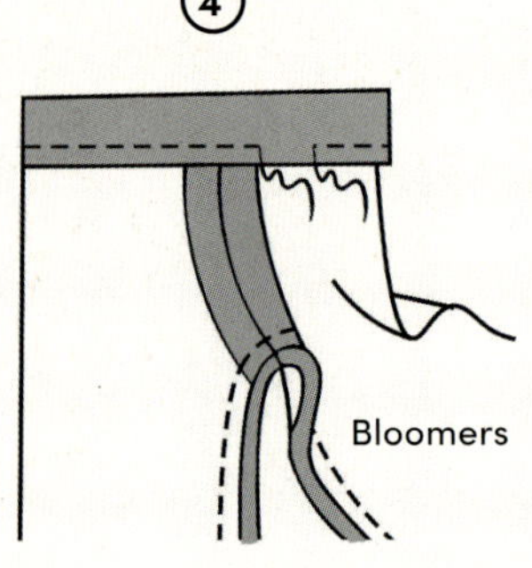

5. Thread the elastic through the zigzag stitching on the legs, making sure there is enough give to fit over the animal's foot, then overlap the ends of the elastic, cut to the required length and stitch the ends together.

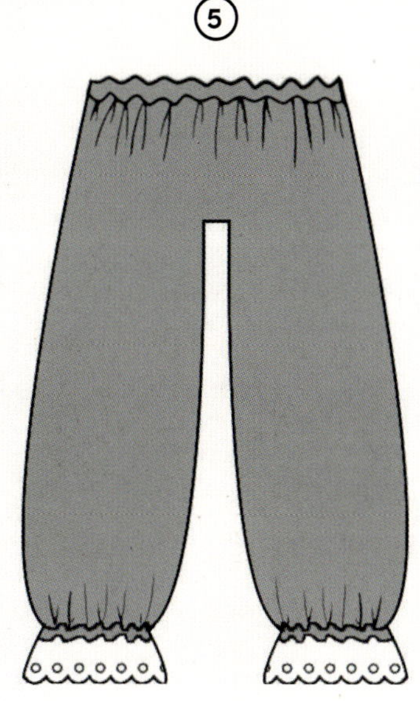

RIBBON BOW VARIATION

Emma and Sapphire's bloomers have pretty little ribbon bows at the waist, tied over the elastic casings.

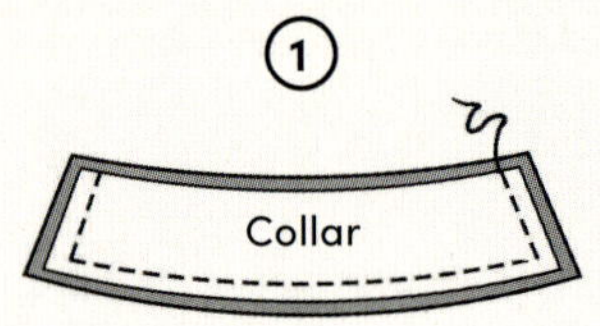

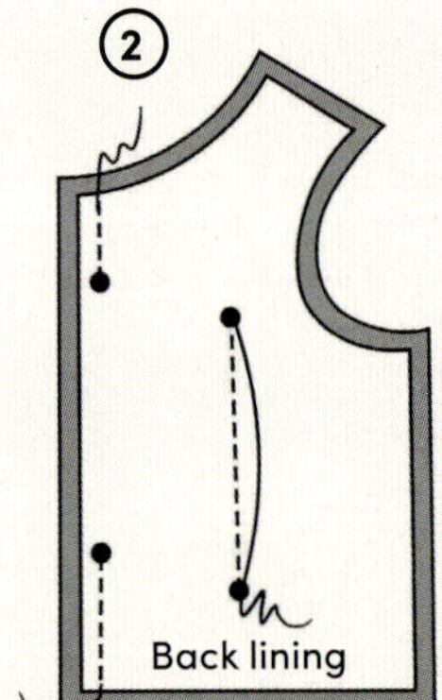

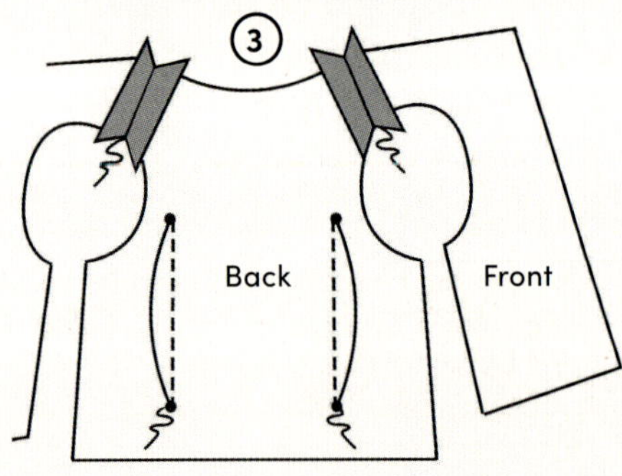

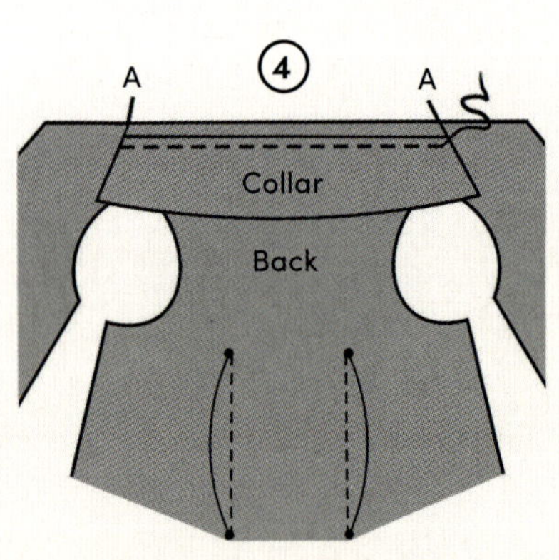

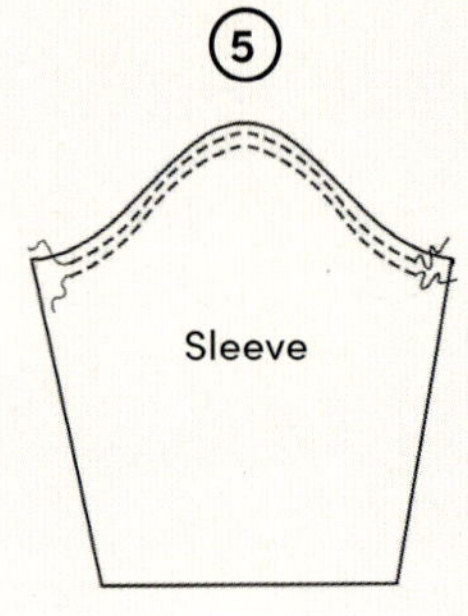

JOSEPHINE JACKET

You will need

- Templates: Front, back, back lining, sleeve, sleeve lining, collar
- 30 x 115cm (12 x 44in) cotton flannel
- 22 x 115cm (8½ x 44in) cotton fabric for lining
- Matching sewing thread
- Stranded embroidery thread (floss)
- 4 x 5mm (3/16in) brass buttons
- 3 x 7mm (¼in) snap fasteners

1. With right sides together, pin and sew the collar pieces together along the short sides and the curved outer edge. Clip the corners, trim the seam allowances and turn right side out. Press.

2. To make the back darts, fold the fabric right sides together between the dots marked on the template, pin and sew in place. Repeat for the back lining. With right sides together, join the two back pieces together. Repeat for the back lining, leaving an opening as indicated on the template.

3. With right sides together, pin and sew the fronts to the back at the shoulder seams. Press the seams open. Repeat for the lining.

4. Tack (baste) the collar to the right side of the jacket between the As marked on the template.

5. Around the sleeve head, sew two rows of gather stitch inside the seam allowance between the points marked on the template.

6. With right sides down, pin the sleeve to the armhole. Pull up the gather stitches gently to fit, spacing the gathers evenly. Tack (baste) and then sew in place. Repeat for the other sleeve and the jacket lining. Trim the seam allowances.

7. With right sides together, pin and sew the underarm and side seams in one continuous line of stitching on each side. Trim the seam allowances. Repeat for the lining.

8. With right sides together, pin and tack (baste) the jacket and lining together. Sew around, trim the seam allowances and turn out through the back opening in the lining. Oversew the lining opening closed.

9. To neaten the sleeves, fold the sleeves and sleeve linings back to the right side of the jacket. Turn the sleeve under by 6mm (¼in) and oversew it to the sleeve.

10. Using three strands of embroidery thread (floss), sew random decorative stitches on the collar, sleeve and bottom edge. Add three buttons to each front and sew snap fasteners behind the buttons to secure.

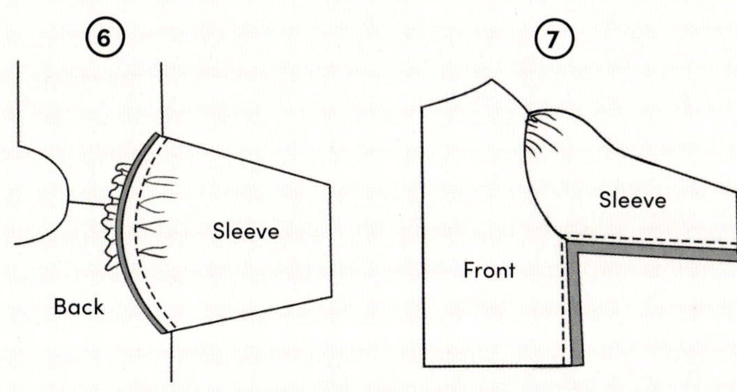

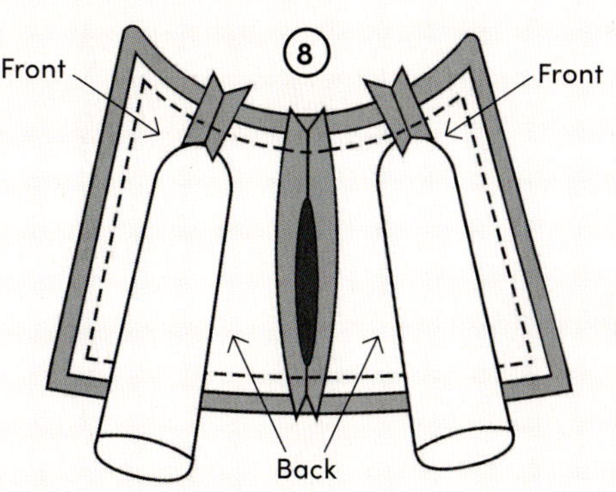

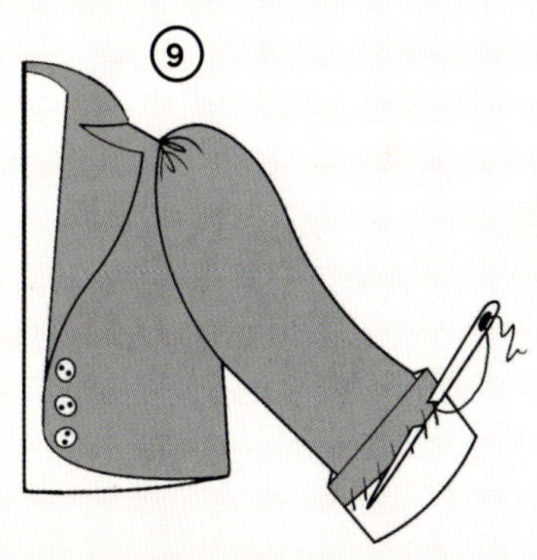

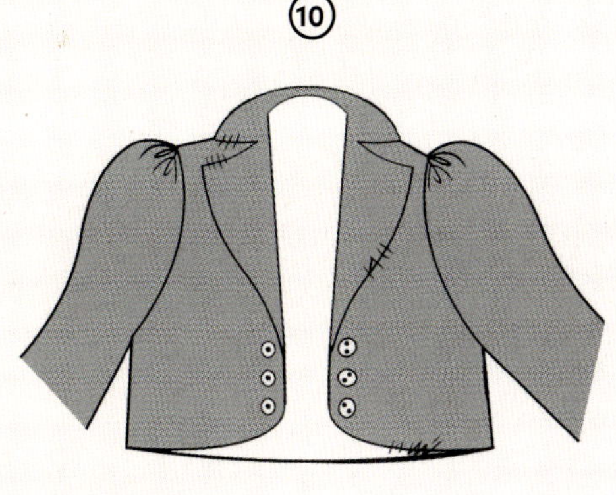

HARRIS JACKET

You will need

- Templates: Front, back, back lining, sleeve, sleeve lining, collar, elbow patch (optional)
- 20 x 60cm (8 x 24in) lightweight woven fabric
- 20 x 60cm (8 x 24in) cotton fabric for lining
- 10 x 50cm (4 x 20in) contrast fabric for patches (optional) and collar
- Matching sewing thread

1. With right sides together, pin and sew the collar pieces together along the short sides and curved outer edge. Clip the corners, trim the seam allowances and turn right side out. Press.

2. With right sides together, pin and sew the two back linings together, leaving an opening as indicated on the template. Trim the seam allowances.

3. With right sides together, pin and sew the fronts to the back at the shoulder seams. Repeat with the lining front and back pieces. Trim the seam allowances and press the seams open.

4. Tack (baste) the collar to the right side of the jacket between the two As marked on the template.

1

Collar

2

Back lining

3

Front

Back

Front

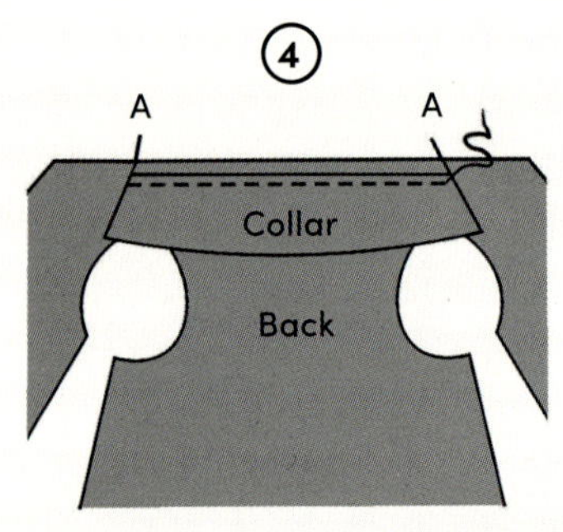

5. Around the sleeve head, sew two rows of gather stitch inside the seam allowance, between the points marked on the template.

6. With right sides down, pin the sleeve to the armhole, pull up the gather stitches gently to fit, tack (baste) and sew in place. Repeat for the other sleeve and the jacket lining. Trim the seam allowances.

7. With right sides together, pin and sew the underarm and side seams in one continuous line of stitching on each side. Repeat with the jacket lining. Trim the seam allowances.

8. With right sides together, pin and tack (baste) the jacket and lining together. Sew around, trim the seam allowances and turn out through the back opening in the lining. Oversew the lining opening together.

9. To neaten the sleeves, fold the sleeves and sleeve lining back to the right side of the sleeve. Turn the sleeve lining under by 6mm (¼in) and oversew it to the sleeve. If you wish, you can add patches to the elbows and blanket stitch them in place.

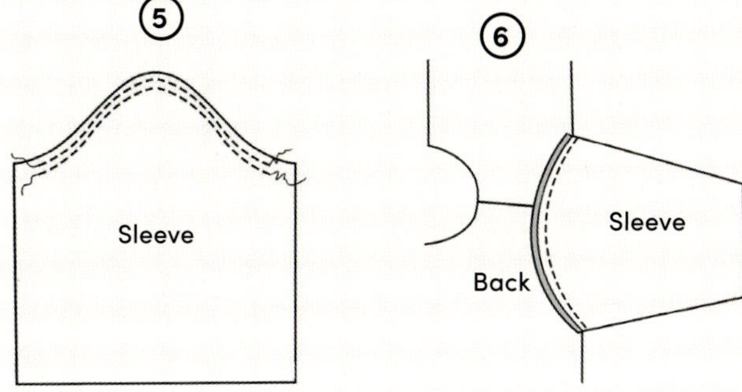

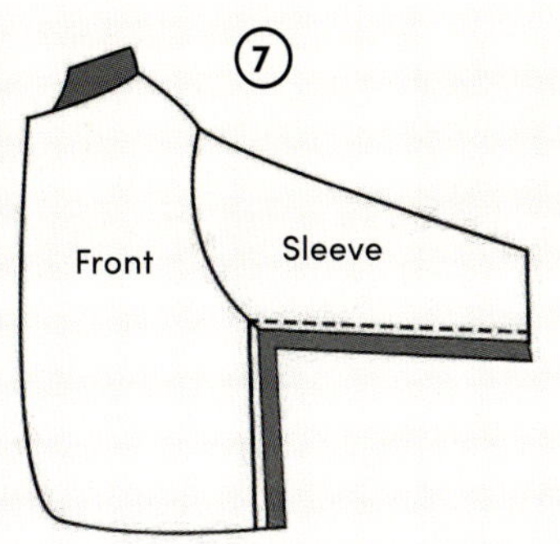

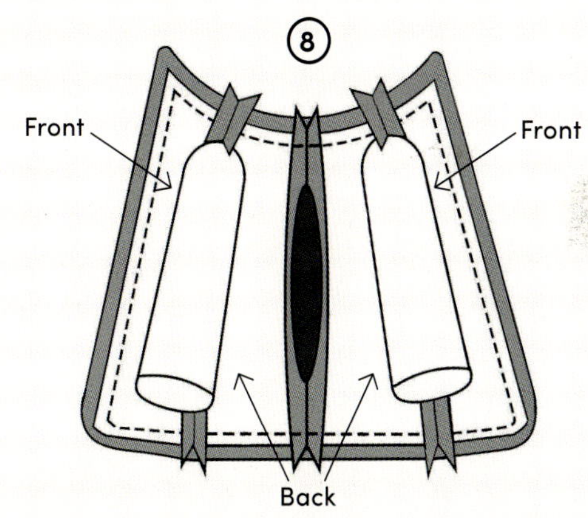

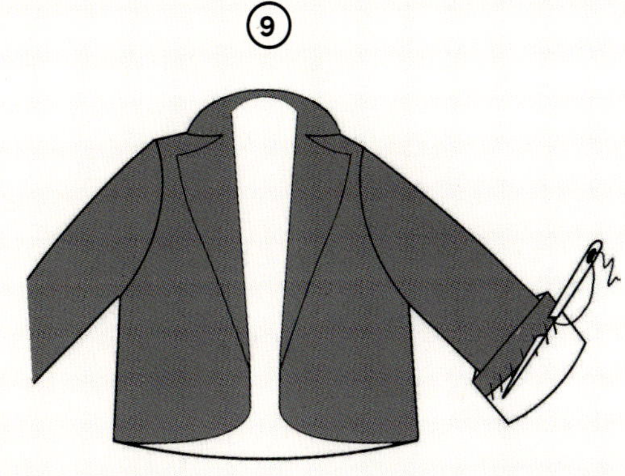

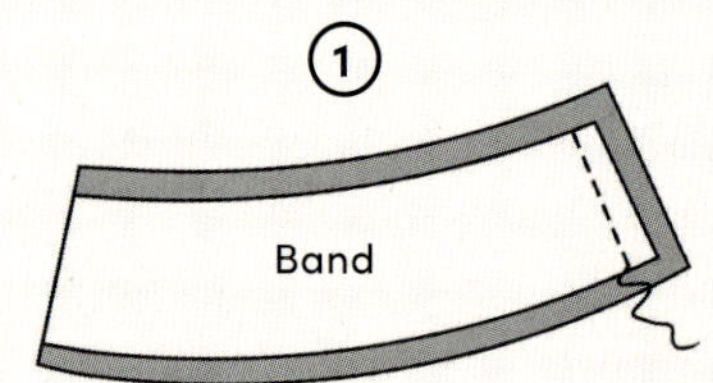

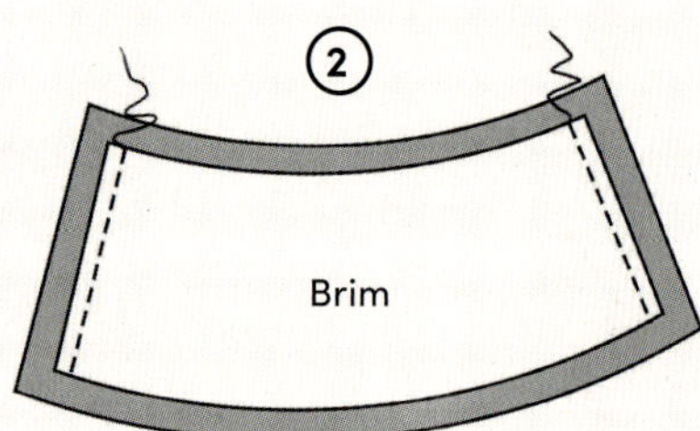

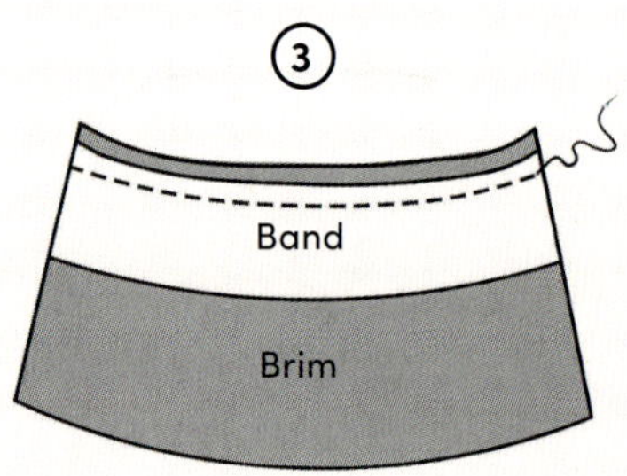

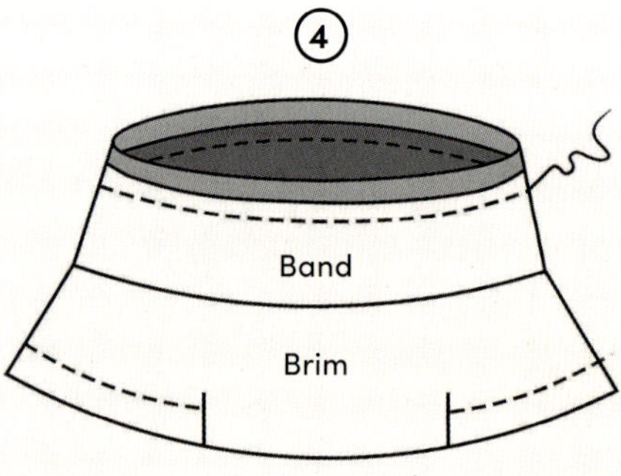

BERRY BRIM HAT

You will need

- Templates: Band, brim, leaf appliqué motif
- 30 x 115cm (12 x 44in) cotton flannel
- 30 x 56cm (12 x 22in) contrast cotton for lining
- 12.5 x 12.5cm (5 x 5in) cotton fabric for appliqué leaves
- 12.5 x 12.5cm (5 x 5in) felt for appliqué leaf surrounds
- 12.5 x 12.5cm (5 x 5in) fusible bonding web
- Matching sewing thread
- 3–5 wired artificial berries, about 1cm (3/8in) in diameter

1. Fold the band in half, right sides together, and pin and sew across the short ends. Trim the seam allowances and turn right side out. Repeat for the contrast fabric piece.

2. Pin the two brim pieces right sides together and sew across the short ends. Trim the seam allowances and turn right side out. Repeat for the contrast fabric pieces.

3. With right sides together, pin the upper edge of the brim to the lower edge of the band and sew together. Trim the seam allowances. Repeat for the contrast fabric pieces.

4. With right sides together, pin and sew the main fabric and contrast fabric together at the top and bottom, leaving an opening on the brim. Trim, turn out through the opening and oversew the opening closed.

5. Trace three leaves onto fusible bonding web and cut out roughly. Following the manufacturer's instructions, apply to the back of your cotton leaf fabric. Cut out the leaves and remove the backing paper from the fusible bonding web. Iron the leaves onto the felt and cut out, leaving a 3mm (⅛in) felt border all around.

6. To finish your Berry Brim Hat, fold up the brim and oversew it onto the band. Sew the leaves onto the hat. Add berries to finish, either oversewing them in place or using a glue gun.

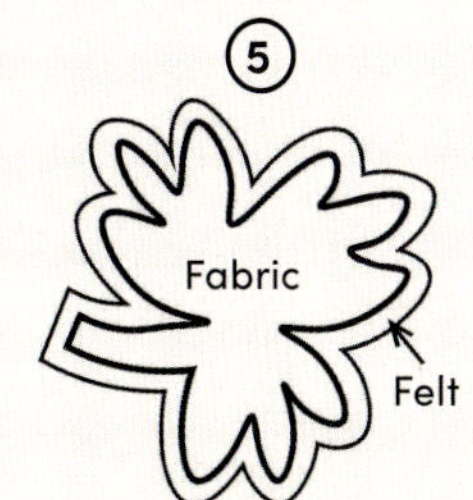

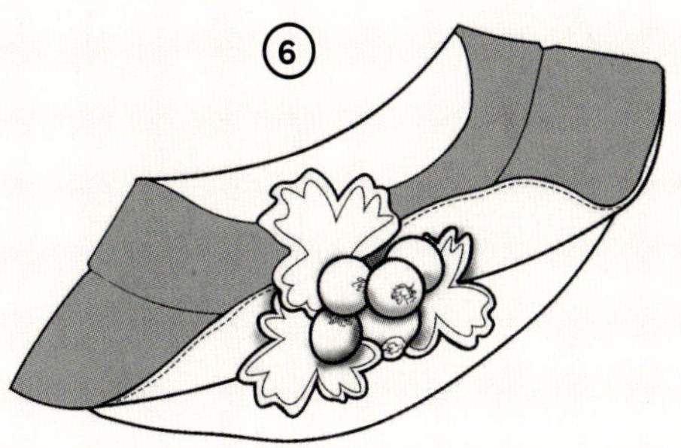

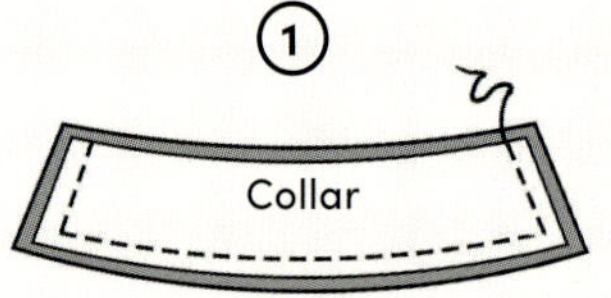

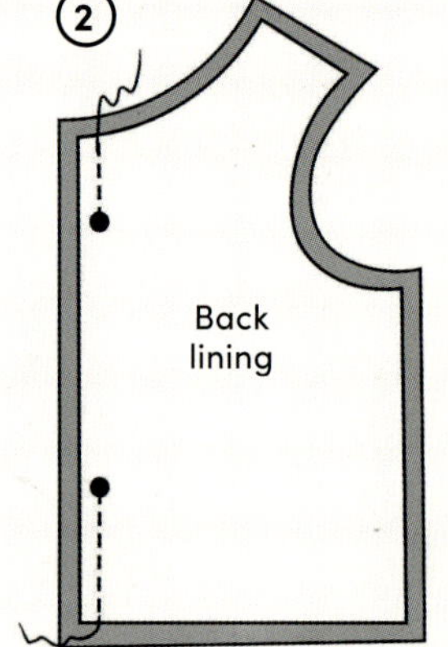

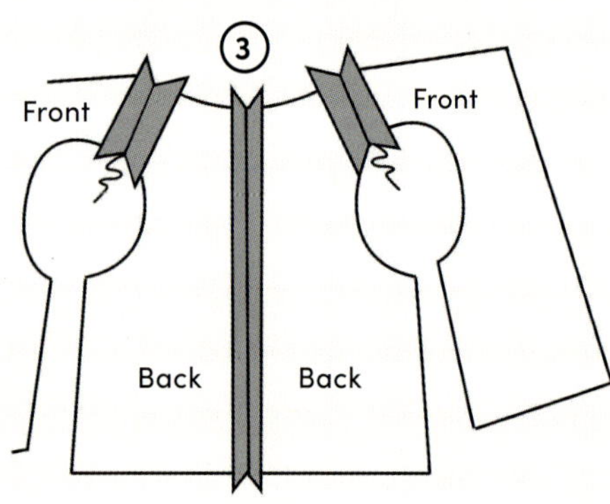

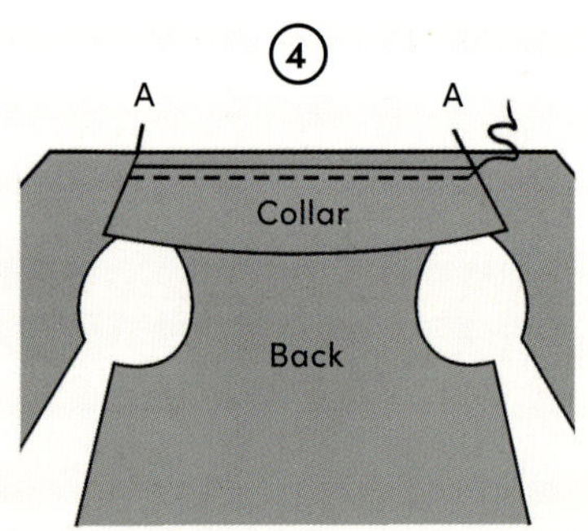

Perfect Petal Jacket

You will need

- Templates: Front, back, back lining, sleeve, peplum, collar
- 25 x 115cm (10 x 44in) lightweight woven fabric
- 25 x 115cm (10 x 44in) cotton fabric for lining
- 30 x 10cm (12 x 4in) contrast fabric for collar
- Matching sewing thread
- 1 x 7mm (¼in) snap fastener
- 1 x 5mm (3/16in) brass button or 6mm (¼in) clasp

1. With right sides together, pin and sew the collar pieces together along the short sides and the curved outer edge. Clip the corners, trim the seam allowances and turn right side out. Press.

2. With right sides together, pin and sew the back lining pieces together, leaving an opening as indicated on the template.

3. With right sides together, pin and sew the fronts to the back at the shoulder seams. Press the seams open. Repeat for the lining.

4. Tack (baste) the collar to the right side of the jacket between the two As marked on the template.

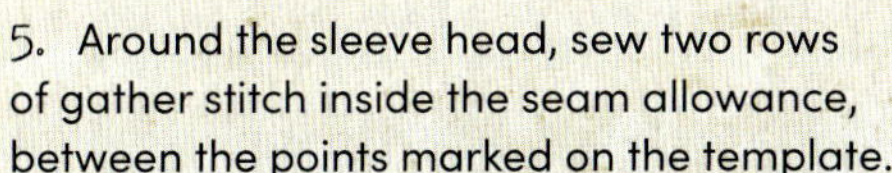

5. Around the sleeve head, sew two rows of gather stitch inside the seam allowance, between the points marked on the template.

6. With right sides down, pin the sleeve to the armhole. Pull up the gather stitches gently to fit, spacing them evenly. Tack (baste) and then sew in place. Repeat for the other sleeve and the jacket lining. Trim the seam allowances.

7. With right sides together, pin and sew the underarm and side seams in one continuous line of stitching on each side. Repeat for the lining. Trim the seam allowances.

8. With right sides together, pin and sew the peplum to the bottom of the jacket. Trim the seam allowances. Repeat for the jacket lining.

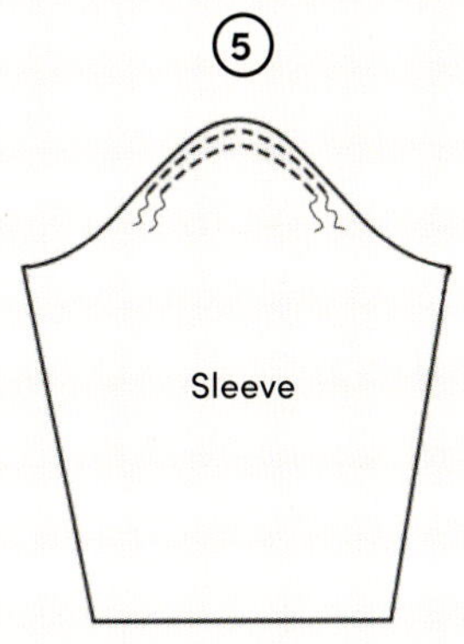

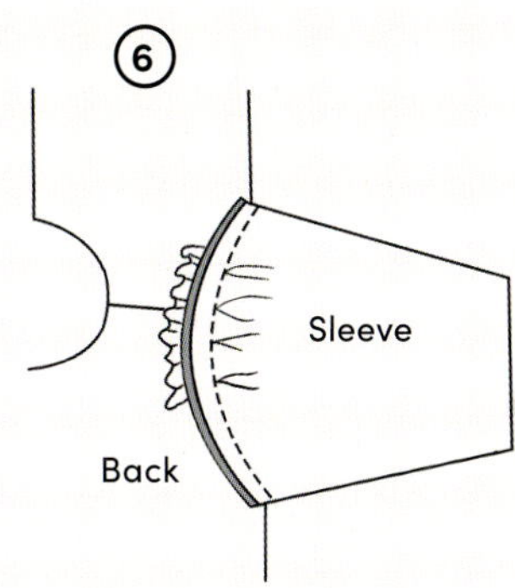

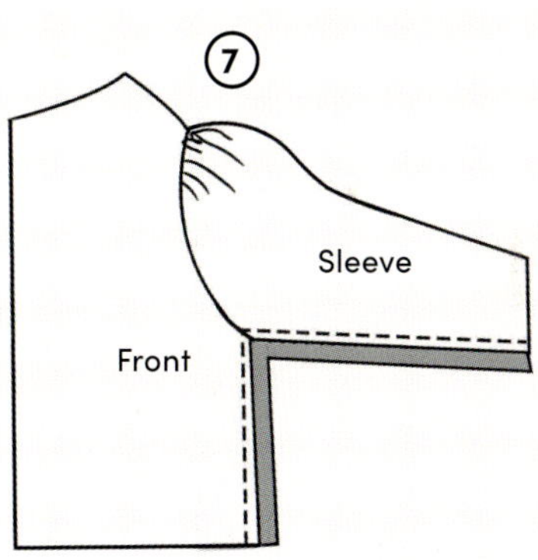

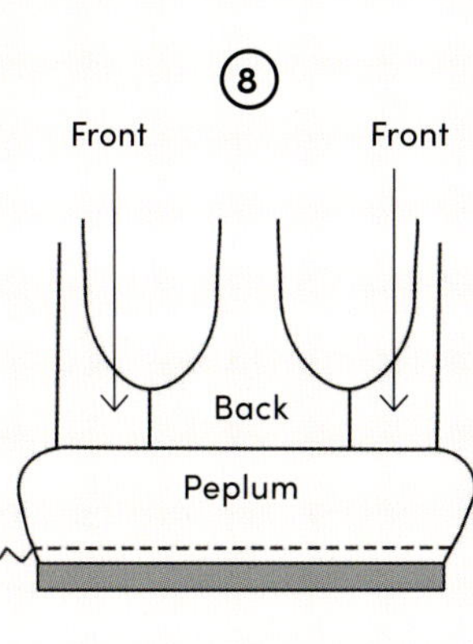

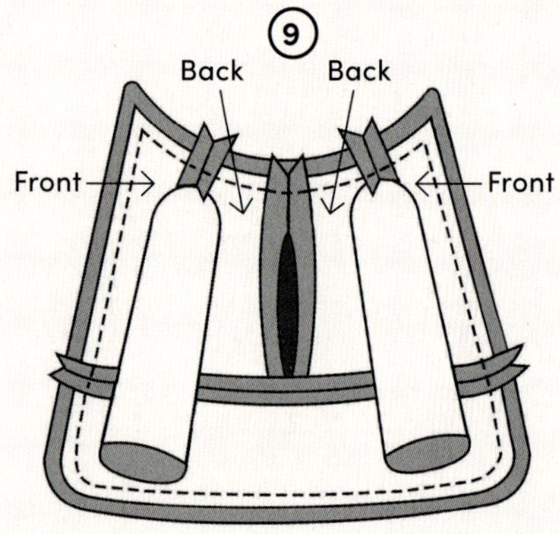

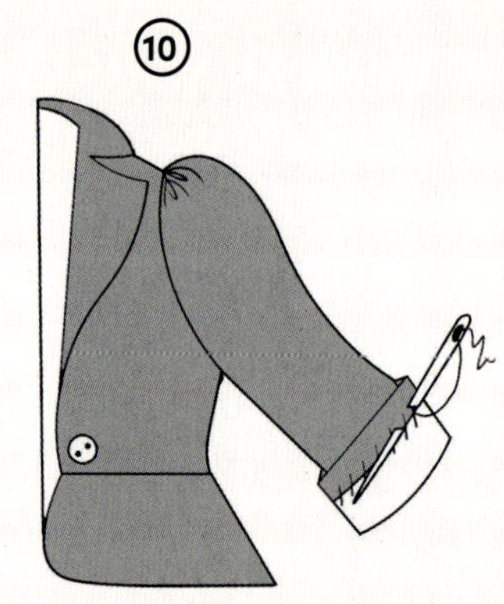

9. With right sides together, pin and tack (baste) the jacket and lining together. Sew around, trim the seam allowances and turn out through the back opening in the lining. Oversew the lining opening together.

10. Fold the sleeves and sleeve lining back to the right side of the sleeve. Turn the sleeve lining under by 6mm (¼in) and oversew it to the sleeve.

11. To finish the jacket, overlap the left front over the right, then sew on a snap fastener and a button or clasp to secure.

MANDARIN WAISTCOAT

You will need

- Templates: Front, back, collar
- 15 x 56cm (6 x 22in) cotton fabric
- 15 x 56cm (6 x 22in) cotton fabric for lining
- Matching sewing thread
- 3 x 5mm (3/16in) brass buttons
- 3 x 7mm (¼in) snap fasteners
- 50cm (20in) crushed ribbon, 6mm (¼in) wide, for necktie

1. With right sides together, pin and sew the collar pieces together along the short sides and the curved outer edge. Clip the corners, trim the seam allowances and turn right side out. Press.

2. To make the back darts, fold the fabric right sides together between the dots marked on the template, pin and sew in place.

3. With right sides together, pin and sew the fronts to the back at the shoulder seams. Press the seams open. Repeat for the lining.

4. Tack (baste) the collar to the right side of the jacket between the As marked on the template.

5. With right sides together, pin and sew the waistcoat and waistcoat lining together, leaving openings where indicated and leaving 6mm (¼in) free from stitching at the side seams. Trim and snip the seam allowances.

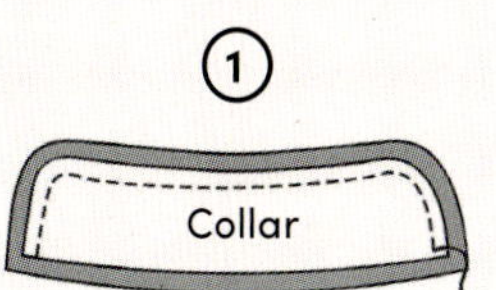

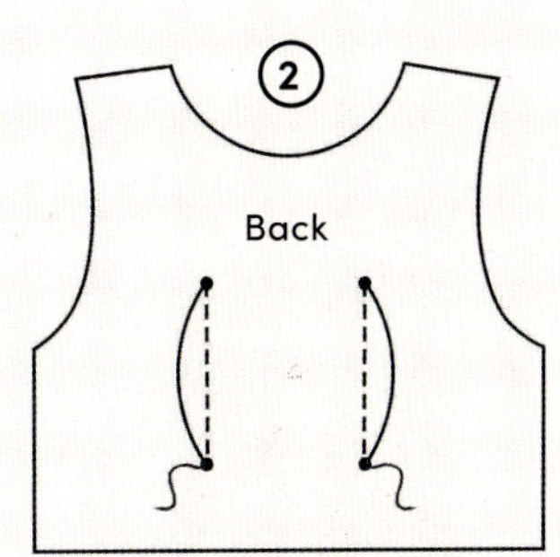

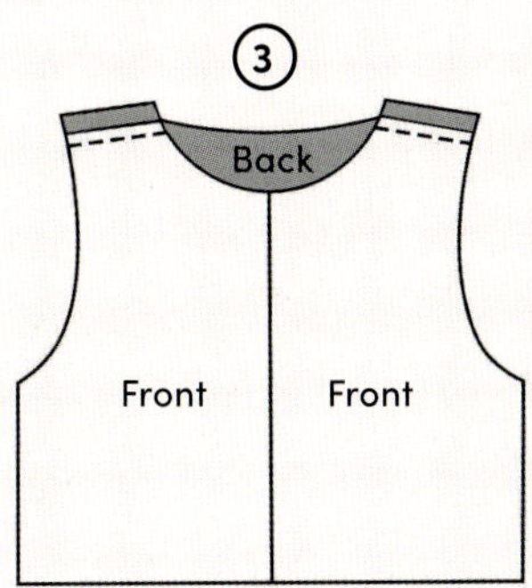

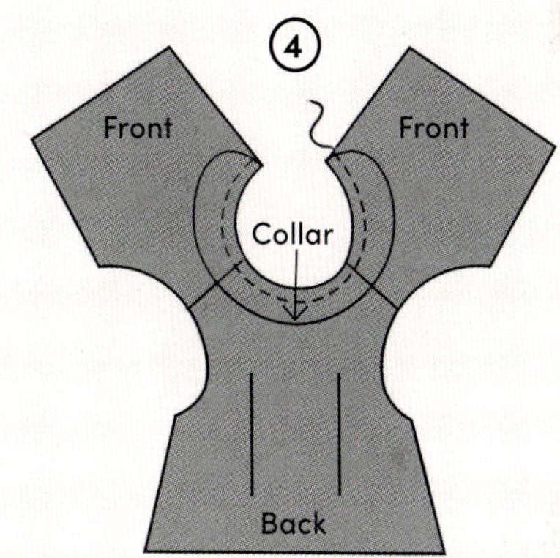

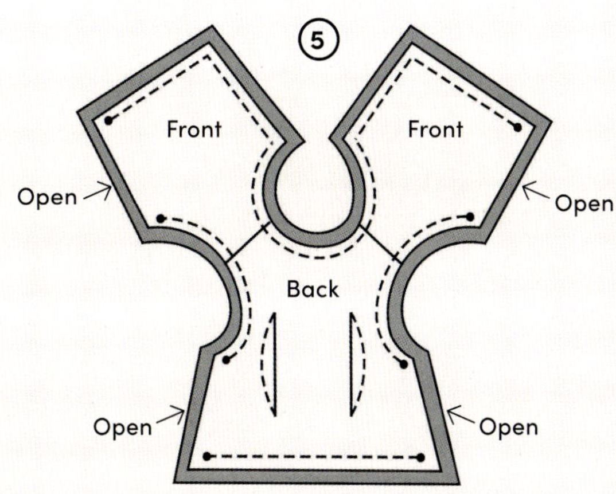

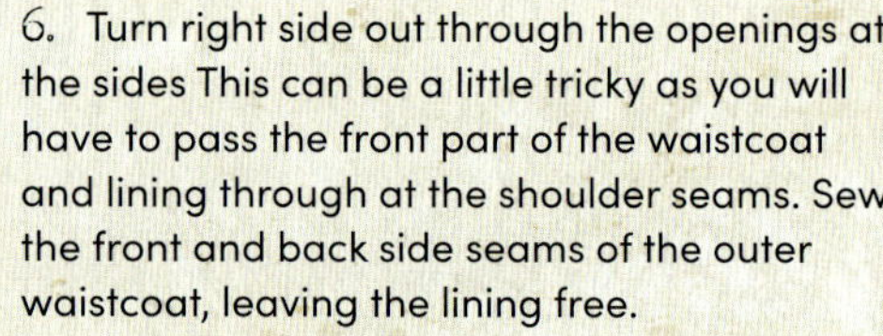

6. Turn right side out through the openings at the sides This can be a little tricky as you will have to pass the front part of the waistcoat and lining through at the shoulder seams. Sew the front and back side seams of the outer waistcoat, leaving the lining free.

7. To neaten the lining, oversew the lining back and front together at the side seams.

8. Add three snap fasteners to the centre front to secure, then stitch a button over each one on the right side. Tie the ribbon in a bow at the neck.

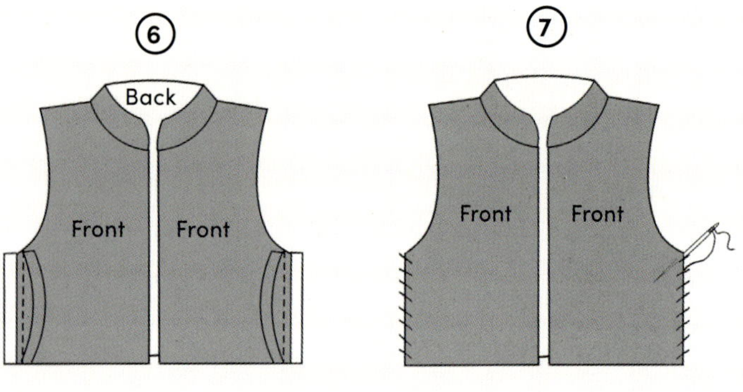

Darcy Trousers

You will need

- Templates: Front leg, back leg, front facing, waistband, pocket
- 30 x 115cm (12 x 44in) cotton fabric
- Matching sewing thread 9 x 5mm (3⁄16in) brass buttons
- 1 x 7mm (¼in) snap fastener

1. To make the darts on the back trouser legs, fold the fabric right sides together between the dots marked on the template, pin and sew in place. Neaten the raw edge on both back trouser openings as far as the dot marked on the template.

2. With right sides together, sew the two front trousers together at the crotch seam. Trim and neaten the seam allowances.

3. With right sides together, sew the facing to the front trouser, following the markings on the facing template. Snip down the middle of both sewn rectangles and into the corners, cutting through both layers. Turn the facing to the wrong side of the trouser through the slits, making sure the corners are neat, and press.

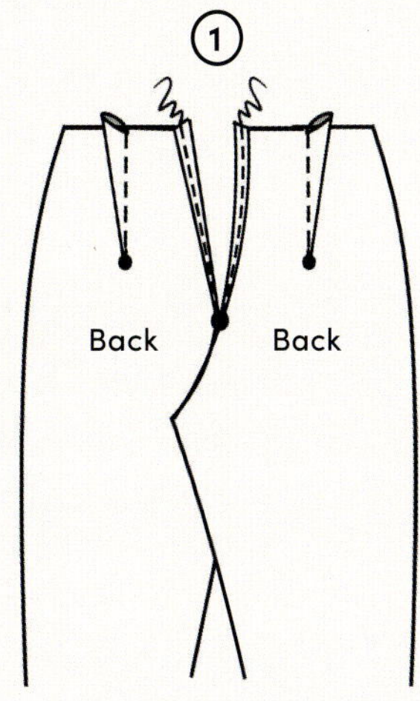

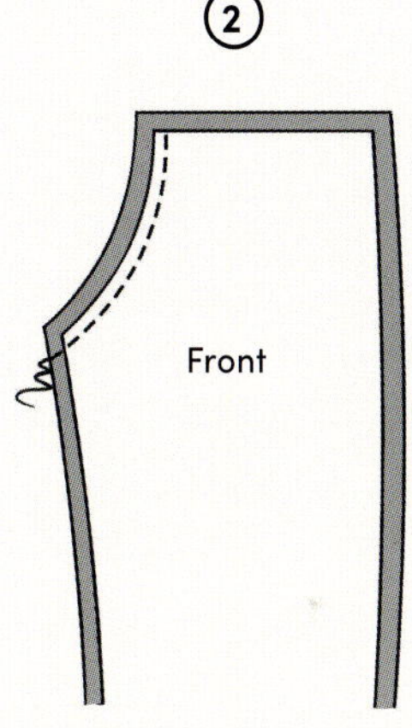

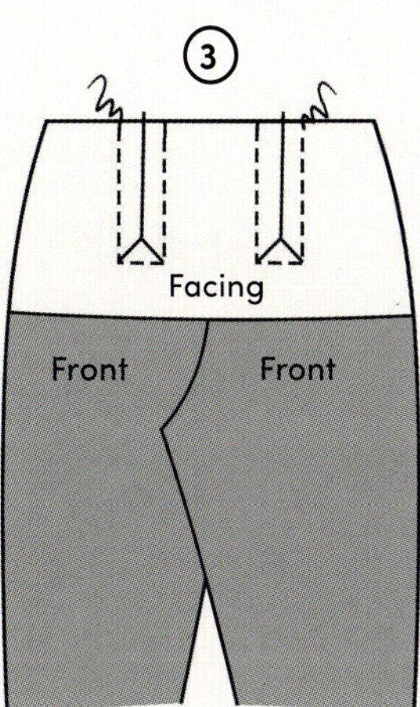

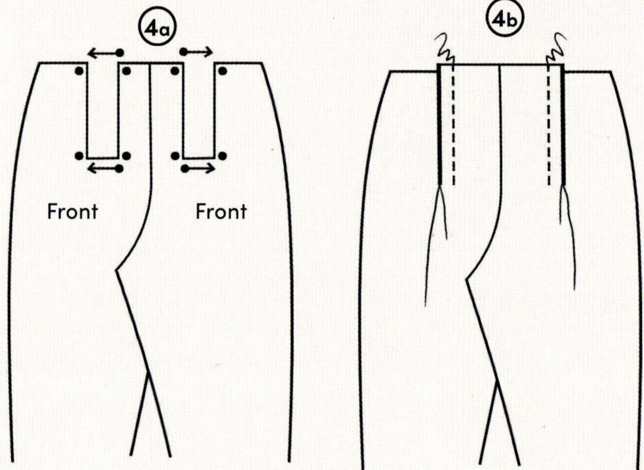

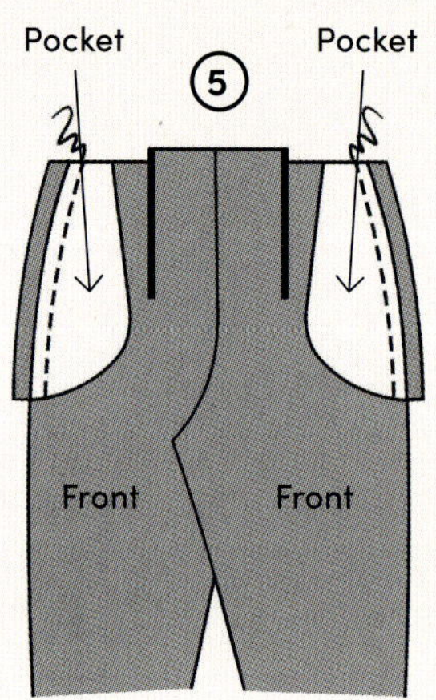

4. With right sides together, fold the open edges of the rectangles on the front facing together in the direction indicated by the arrows on the template. Pin and tack (baste) in place.

5. With right sides together, pin and sew a pocket piece to each front trouser leg. Press the pockets outwards, away from the trouser legs.

6. With right sides together, pin and sew a pocket piece to each back trouser leg. With right sides together, pin and sew the back trouser legs together from the crotch to the dot on the back trouser opening. Press the pockets outwards, away from the trouser legs.

7. With right sides together, pin the back and front trousers together at the sides and sew from top of the pockets right down the outside side of both legs. Now pin and sew the inside leg seams. Trim, neaten the seam allowances and turn right side out.

8. With wrong sides together, press the waistband in half widthways. Pin the waistband around the top of the trousers, right sides together, and sew in place around the top edge. One side should be flush with the trouser opening and the other side should extend beyond it, to allow space to attach a snap fastener. Press the waistband up, away from the trousers.

9. Fold the waistband along the crease made in step 8. Fold the raw edge of the waistband under and press, making sure the waistband is a consistent width all the way around. Oversew in place. Add a button and a snap fastener to the open back of the trouser to secure.

10. To finish the trousers add four buttons on each side of the front detail, through both layers. Remove the tacking (basting) stitches. Pop the trousers on your animal, pin the trouser legs up to desired length, make a double fold and oversew the hem in place.

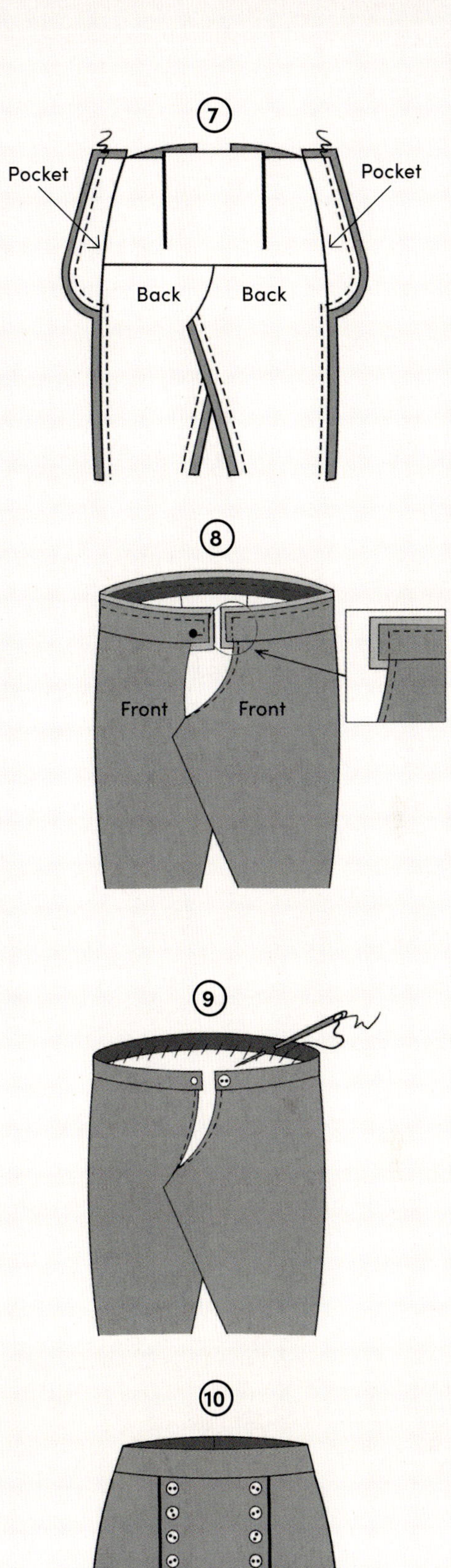

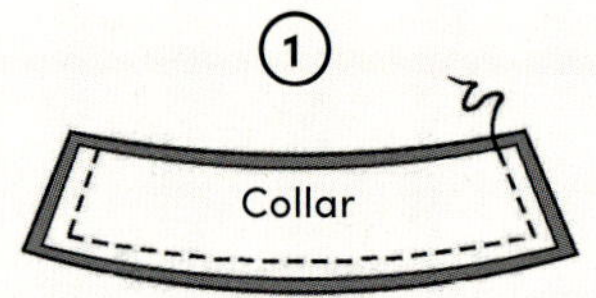

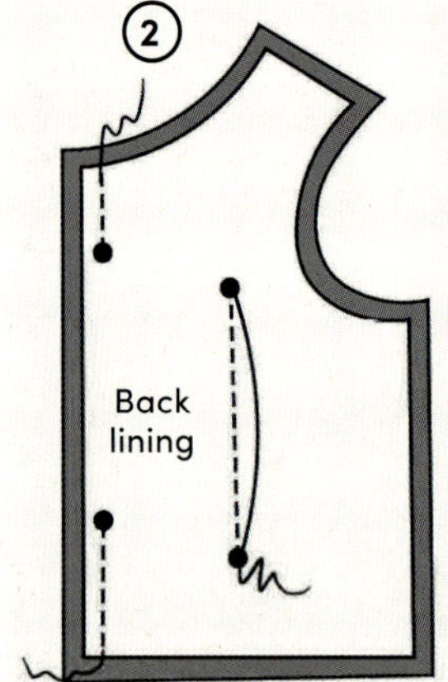

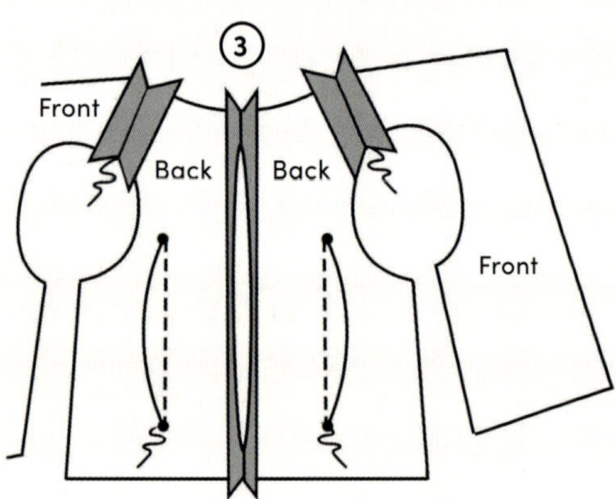

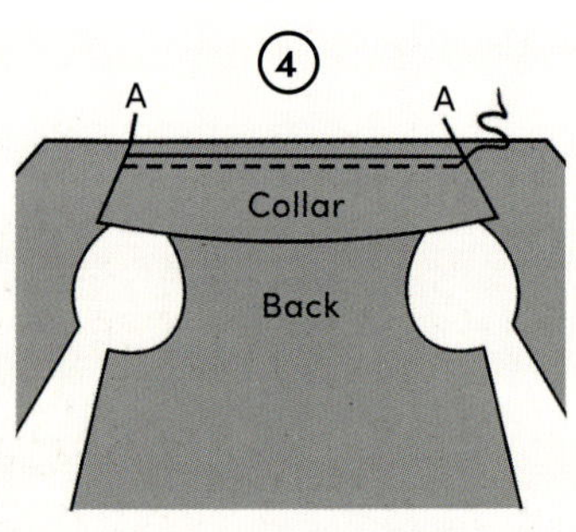

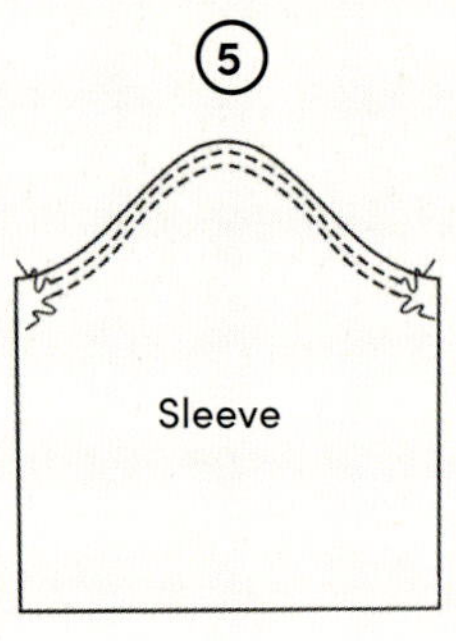

Regency Jacket

You will need

- Templates: Front, back, back lining, sleeve, sleeve lining, collar
- 20 x 115cm (8 x 44in) lightweight woven fabric
- 20 x 115cm (8 x 44in) cotton fabric for lining
- Matching sewing thread

1. With right sides together, pin and sew the collar pieces together along the short sides and the curved outer edge. Clip the corners, trim the seam allowances and turn right side out. Press.

2. To make the back darts, fold the fabric right sides together between the dots marked on the template, pin and sew in place. Repeat for the back lining. With right sides facing, join the two back lining pieces together leaving an opening as indicated on the templates. Repeat for the back lining.

3. With right sides together, pin and sew the fronts to the back at the shoulder seams. Press the seams open. Repeat for the lining.

4. Tack (baste) the collar to the right side of the jacket between the As marked on the template.

5. Around the sleeve head, sew two rows of gather stitch inside the seam allowance between the points marked on the template.

6. With right sides down, pin the sleeve to the armhole. Pull up the gather stitches gently to fit, spacing them evenly. Tack (baste) and then sew in place. Repeat for the other sleeve and the jacket lining. Trim the seam allowances.

7. With right sides together, pin and sew the underarm and side seams in one continuous line of stitching on each side. Repeat for the lining. Trim the seam allowances.

8. With right sides together, pin and tack (baste) the jacket and lining together. Sew around, trim the seam allowances and turn out through the back opening in the lining. Oversew the lining opening together.

9. Fold the sleeves and sleeve lining back to the right side. Turn the sleeve lining under by 6mm (¼in) and oversew it to the sleeve.

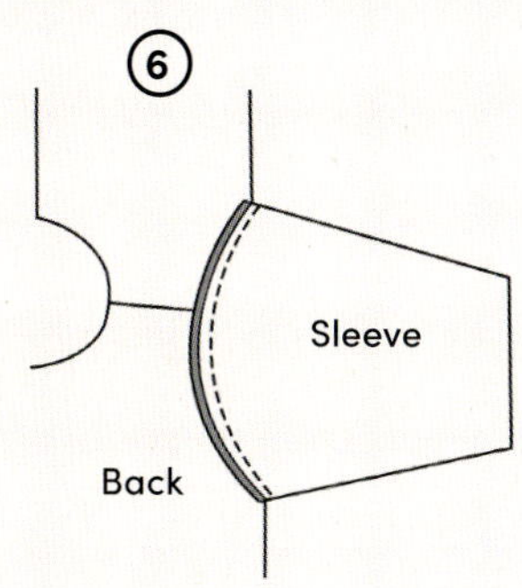

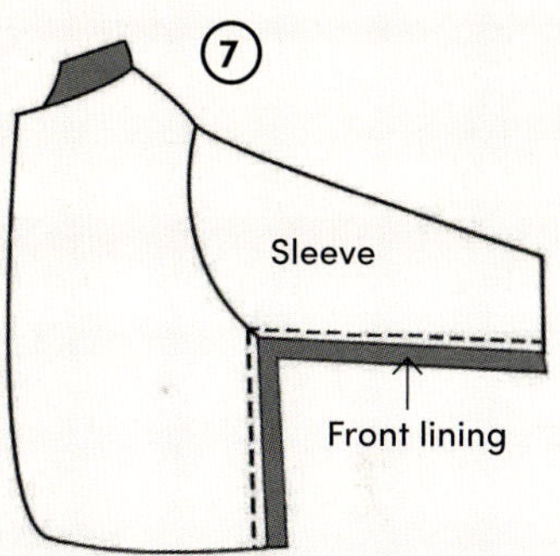

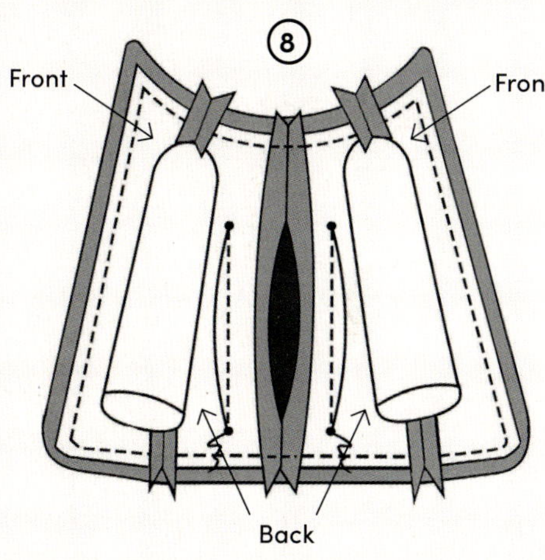

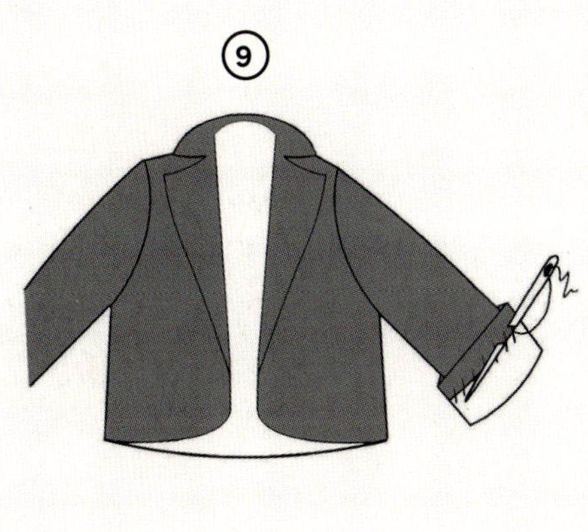

Templates

All the templates for the animals and their wardrobes are full size, so you can just trace them onto card, ready to use.

Fold your fabric in half, with right sides together for the animals' clothes, as you'll be using a woven or a printed fabric. (Felt, which is used for all the animals' bodies, doesn't have a 'right' or a 'wrong' side.) This means you'll be drawing on the wrong side – so if your marks don't come off, they won't show on the finished piece. It also means that where you need to cut two copies of the same template (the left front and right front of a shirt, for example), you'll get two identical pieces.

Now cut out the templates you need for each animal or garment – they're all listed in the instructions. Place them on your folded fabric, leaving at least 1cm (3/8in) space between them. Draw around each template in turn and copy any markings such as darts or dots to show where you leave a gap in the stitching.

Now you can cut out the pieces – but unless the template says otherwise, cut roughly 6mm (1/4in) beyond your drawn lines. This extra fabric is your seam allowance.

When you're ready to sew pieces together, sew on the drawn line – and your pieces will match up perfectly every time!

UNIVERSAL ANIMAL

Add 6mm (¼in) seam allowance unless otherwise indicated.

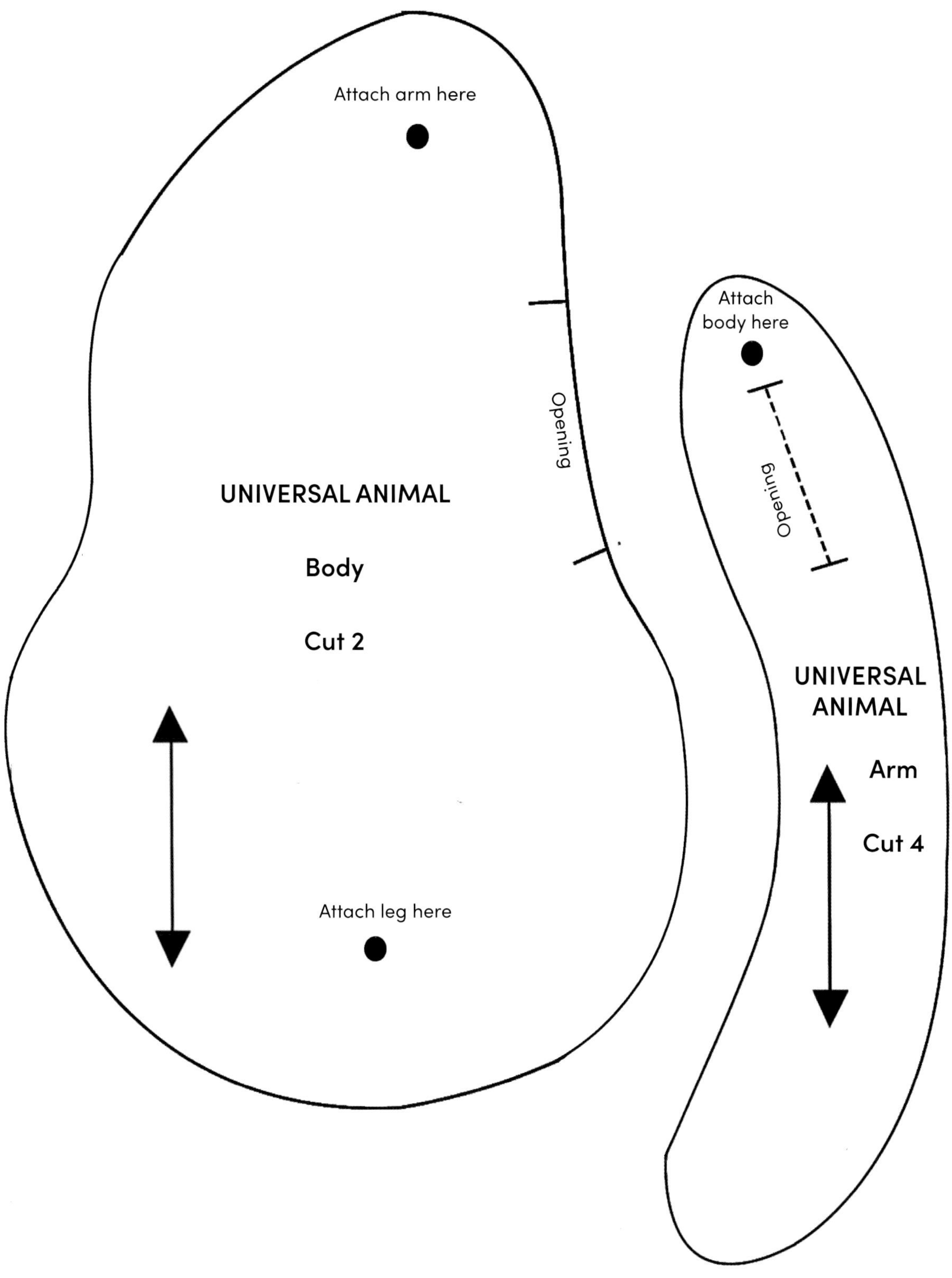

UNIVERSAL ANIMAL

Add 6mm (¼in) seam allowance unless otherwise indicated.

BEAR

Add 6mm (¼in) seam allowance unless otherwise indicated.

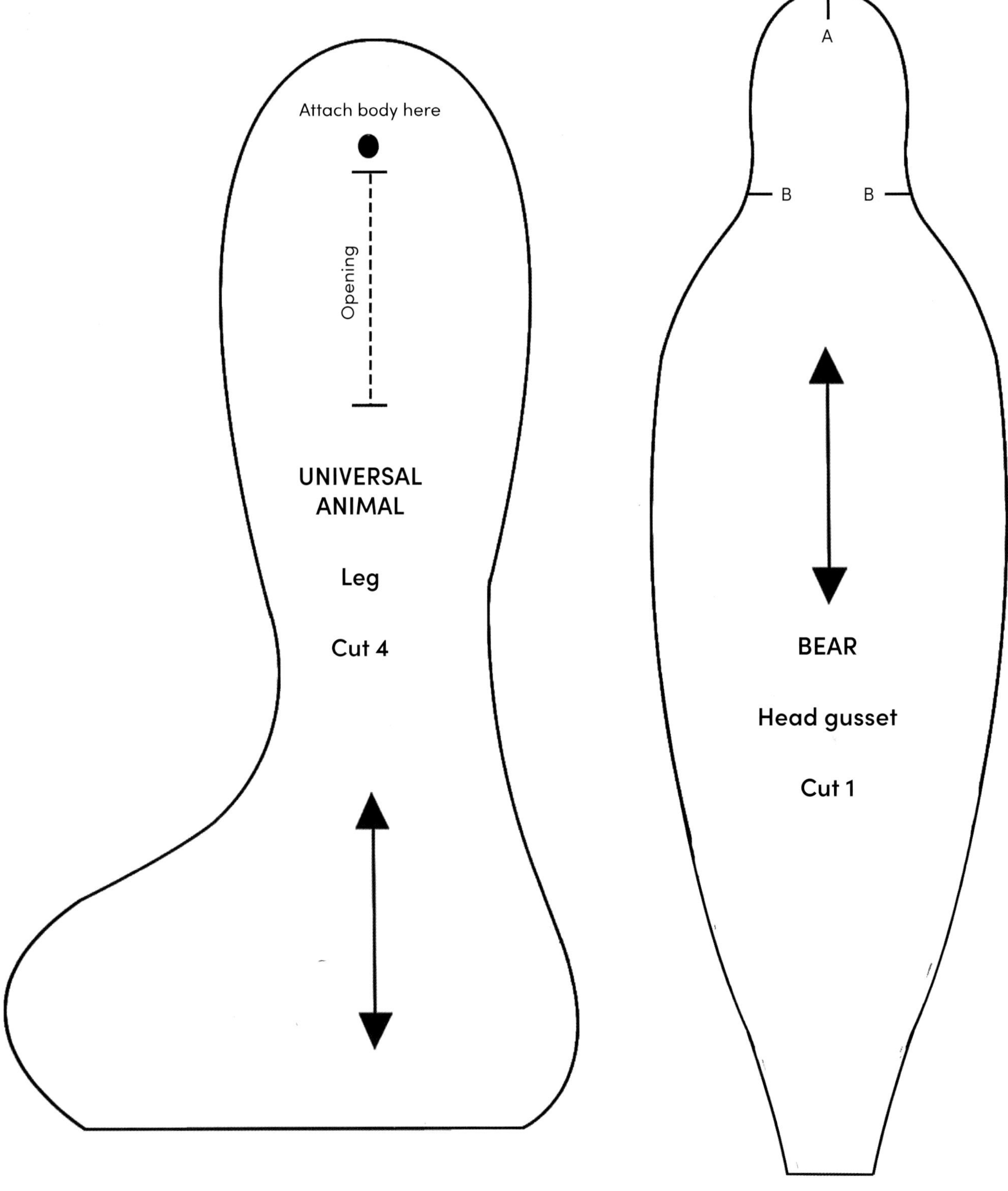

BEAR

Add 6mm (¼in) seam allowance unless otherwise indicated.

ELEPHANT

Add 6mm (¼in) seam allowance unless otherwise indicated.

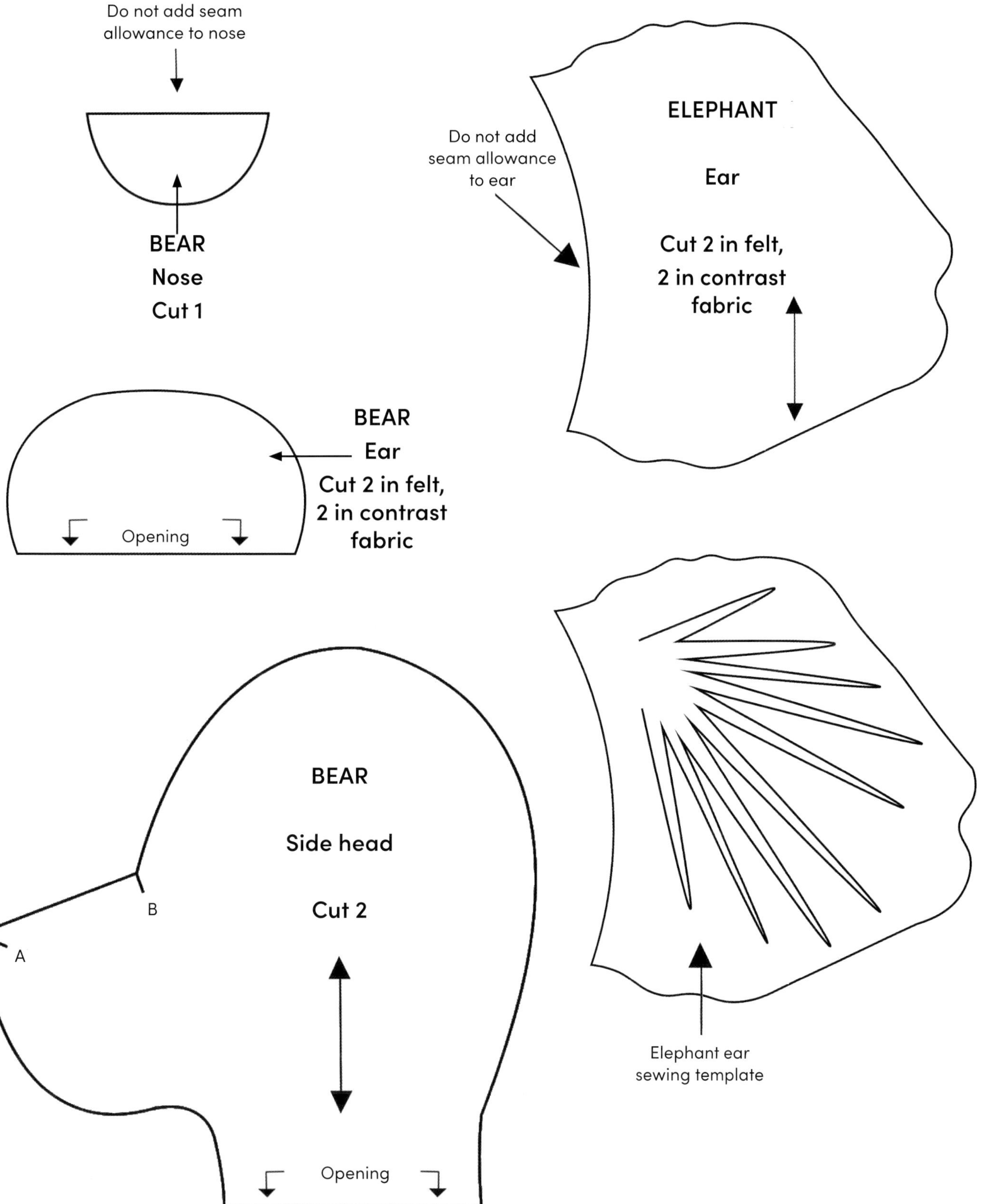

ELEPHANT

Add 6mm (¼in) seam allowance unless otherwise indicated.

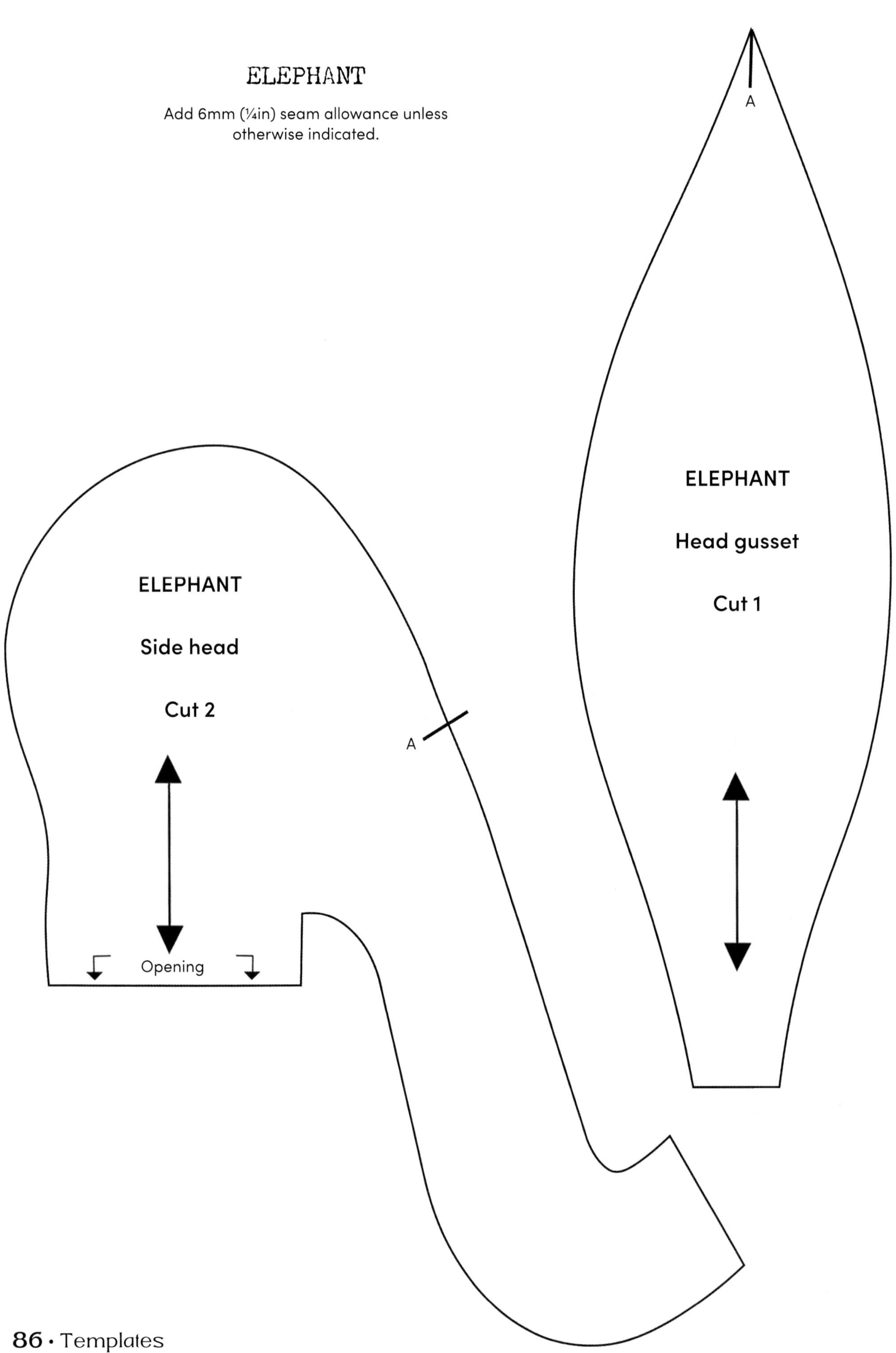

FOX

Add 6mm (¼in) seam seam allowance unless otherwise indicated.

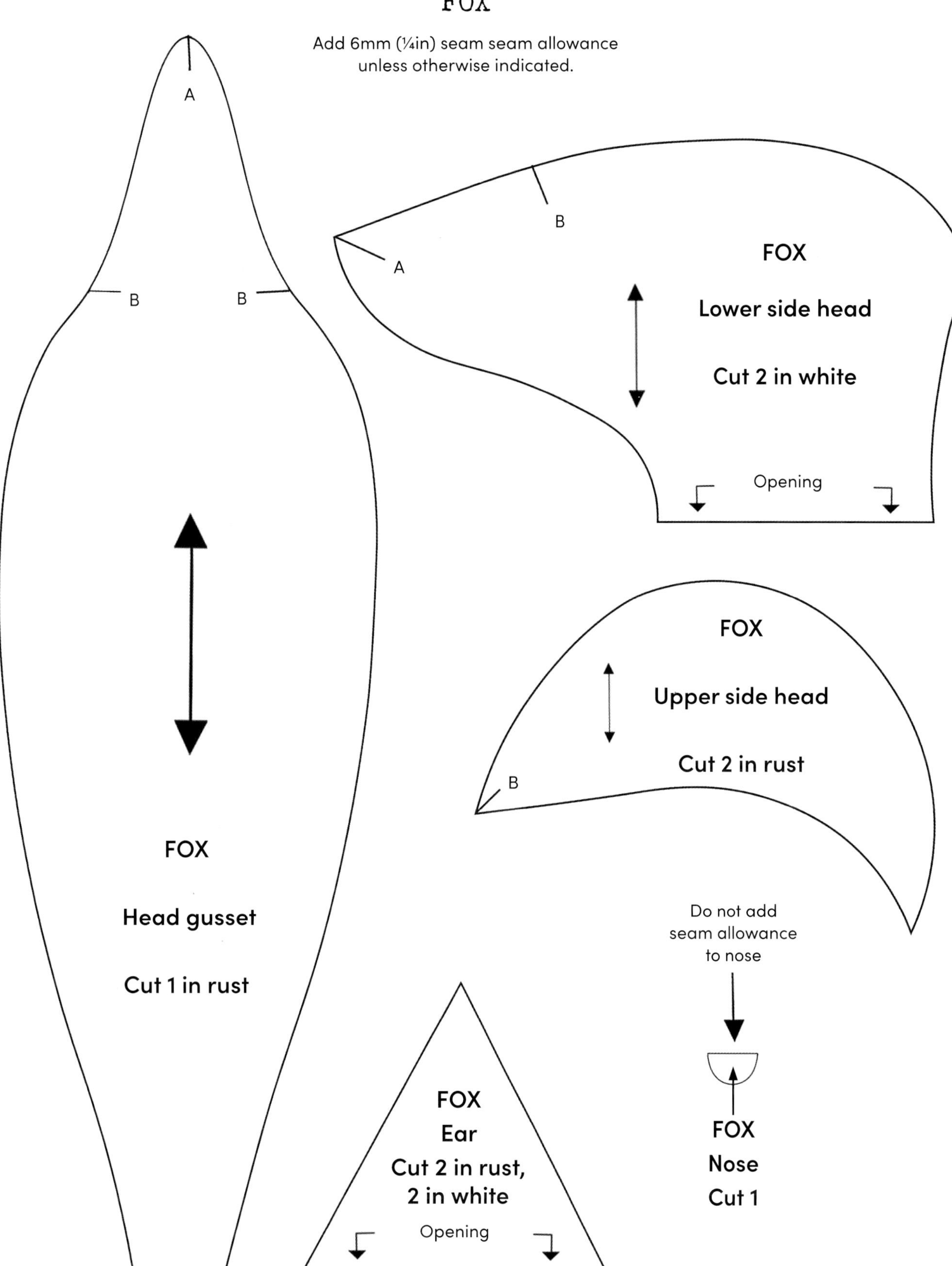

HIGHLAND COW

Add 6mm (¼in) seam allowance unless otherwise indicated.

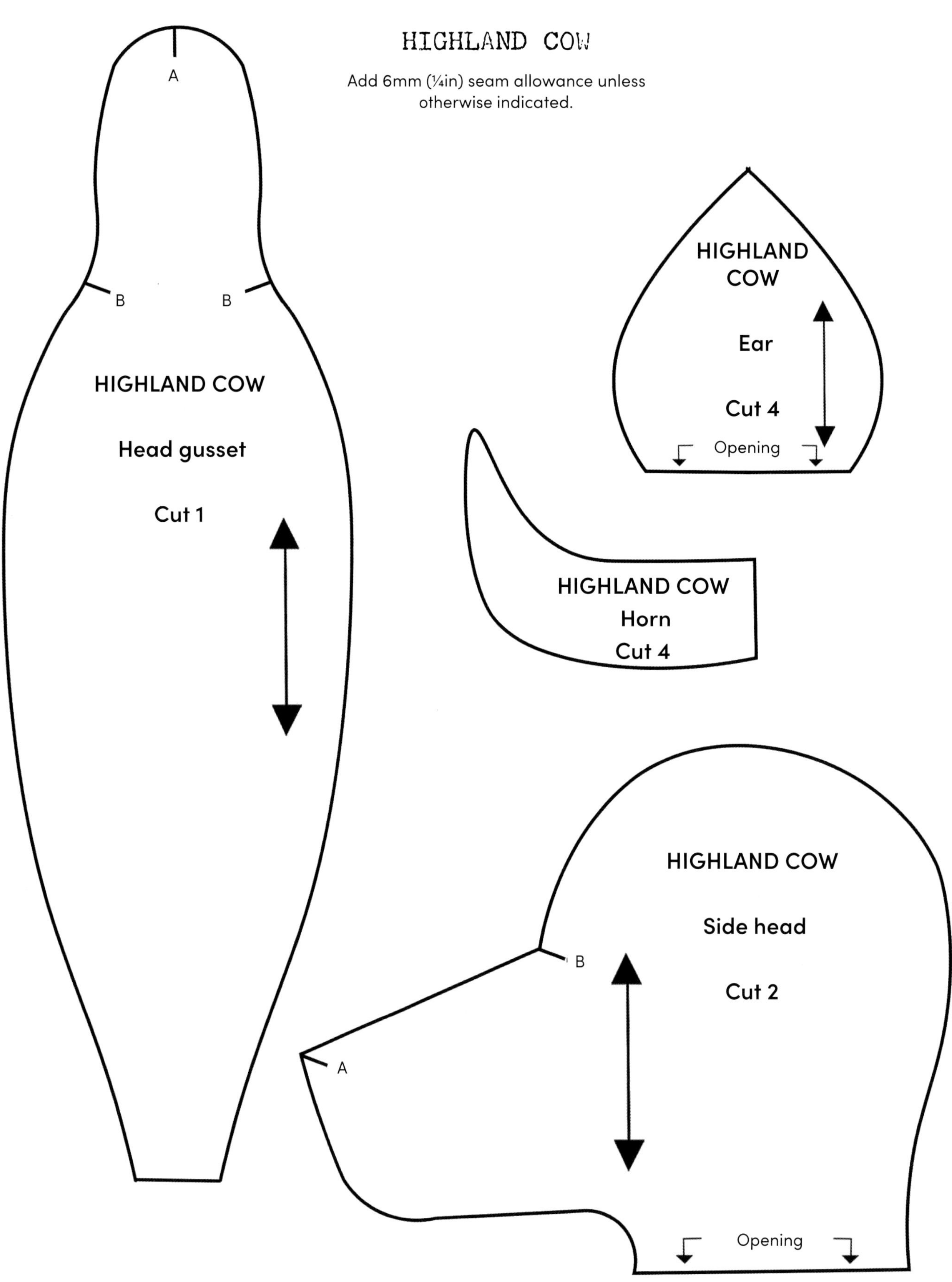

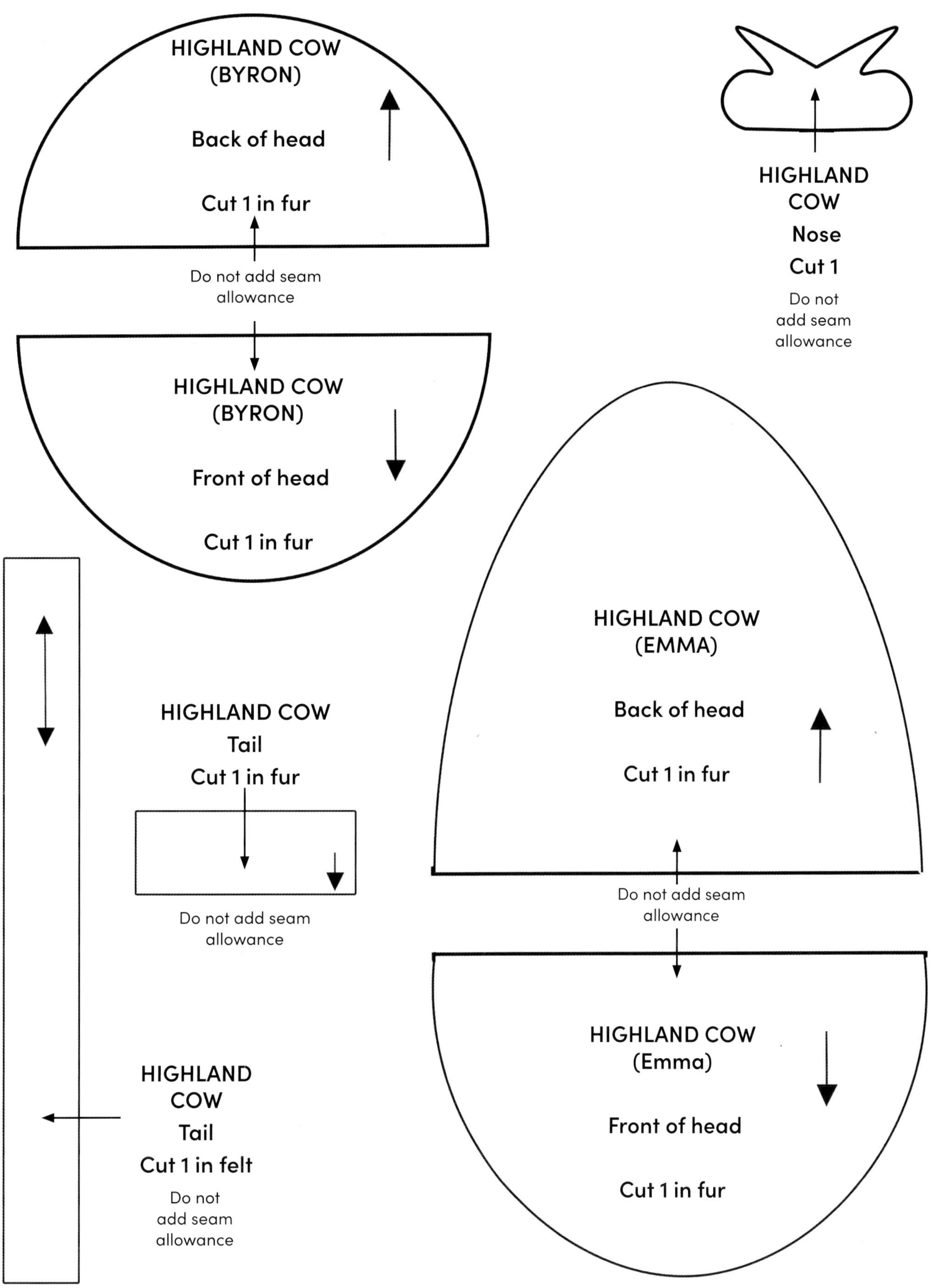
HIGHLAND COW
(BYRON)
Back of head
Cut 1 in fur
Do not add seam allowance
HIGHLAND COW
(BYRON)
Front of head
Cut 1 in fur
HIGHLAND COW
Nose
Cut 1
Do not add seam allowance
HIGHLAND COW
Tail
Cut 1 in fur
Do not add seam allowance
HIGHLAND COW
(EMMA)
Back of head
Cut 1 in fur
Do not add seam allowance
HIGHLAND COW
(Emma)
Front of head
Cut 1 in fur
HIGHLAND COW
Tail
Cut 1 in felt
Do not add seam allowance

AUSTEN WAISTCOAT

Add 6mm (¼in) seam allowance unless otherwise indicated.

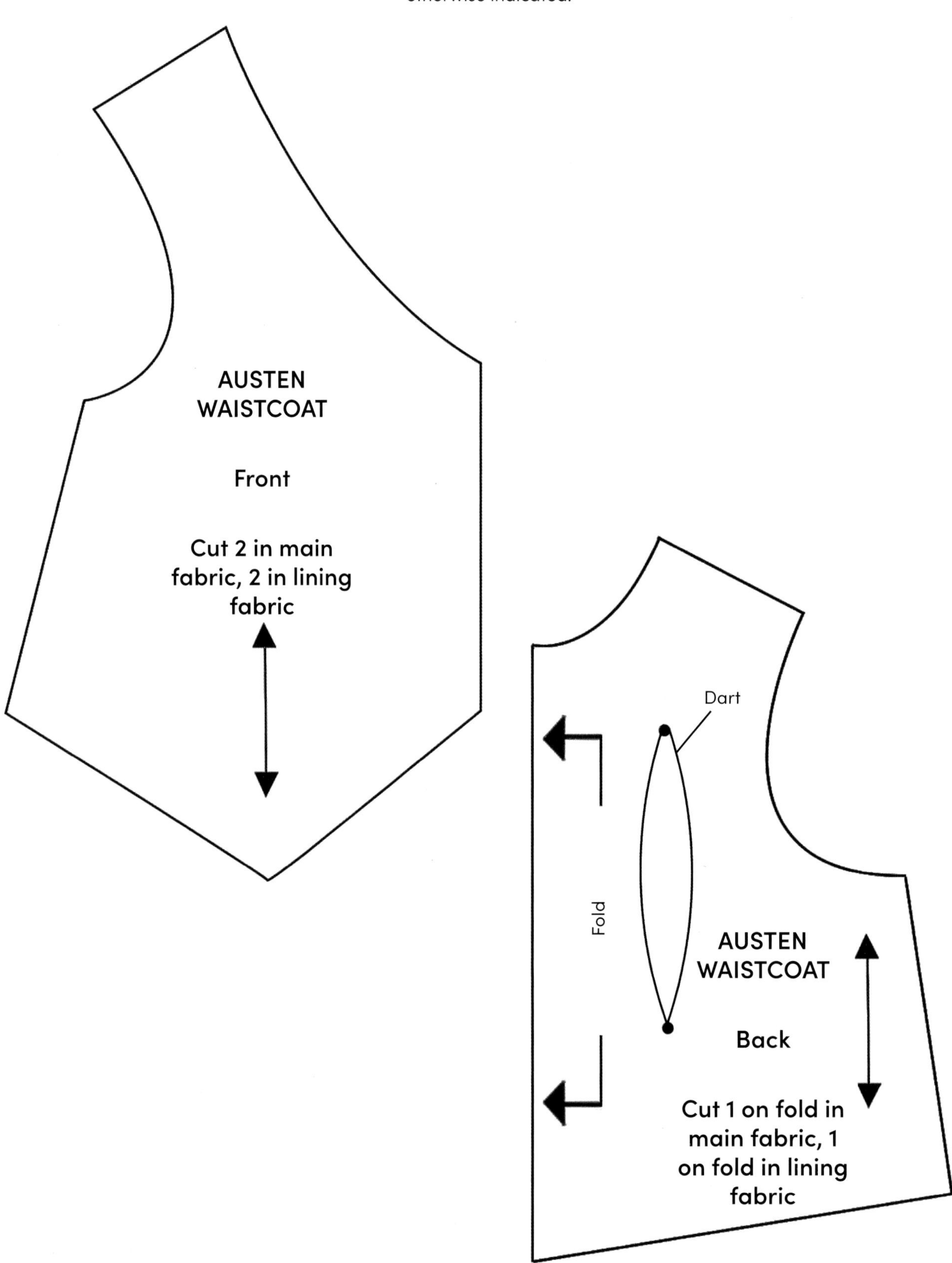

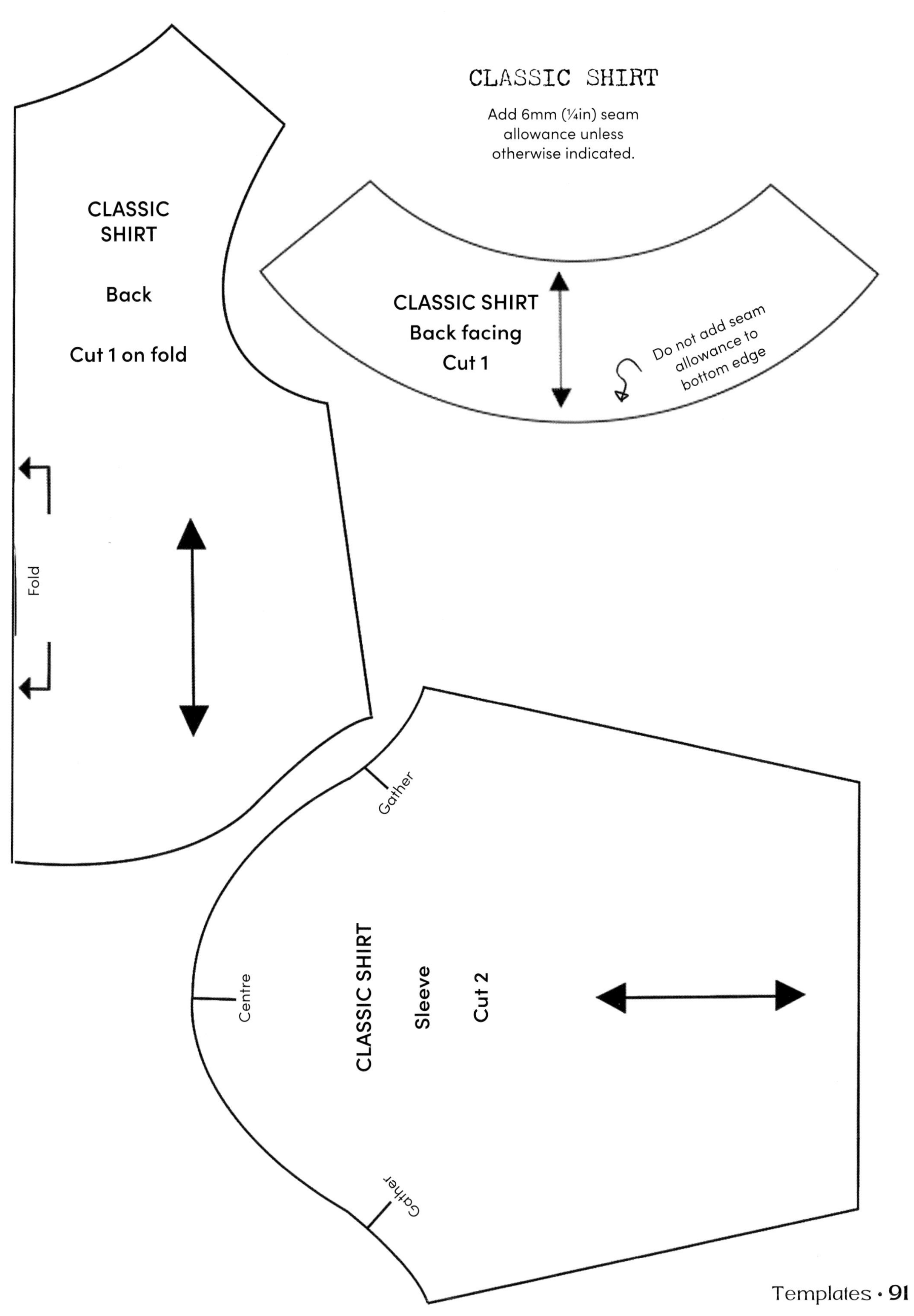

CLASSIC SHIRT
Add 6mm (¼in) seam allowance unless otherwise indicated.
CLASSIC SHIRT
Back
Cut 1 on fold
Fold
CLASSIC SHIRT
Back facing
Cut 1
Do not add seam allowance to bottom edge
Gather
CLASSIC SHIRT
Sleeve
Cut 2
Centre
Gather

CLASSIC SHIRT

Add 6mm (¼in) seam allowance unless otherwise indicated.

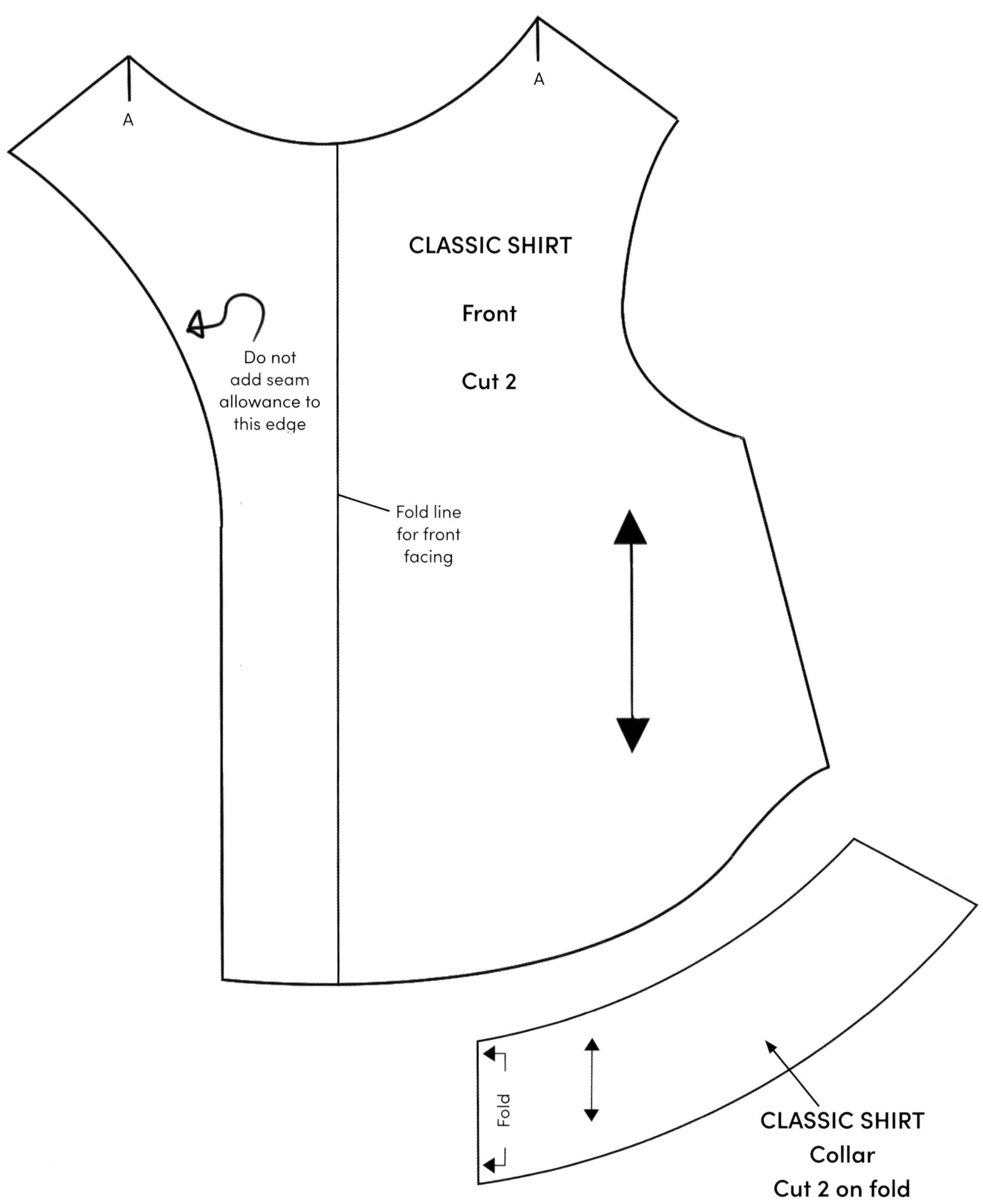

CLASSIC TROUSERS

Add 6mm (¼in) seam allowance unless otherwise indicated.

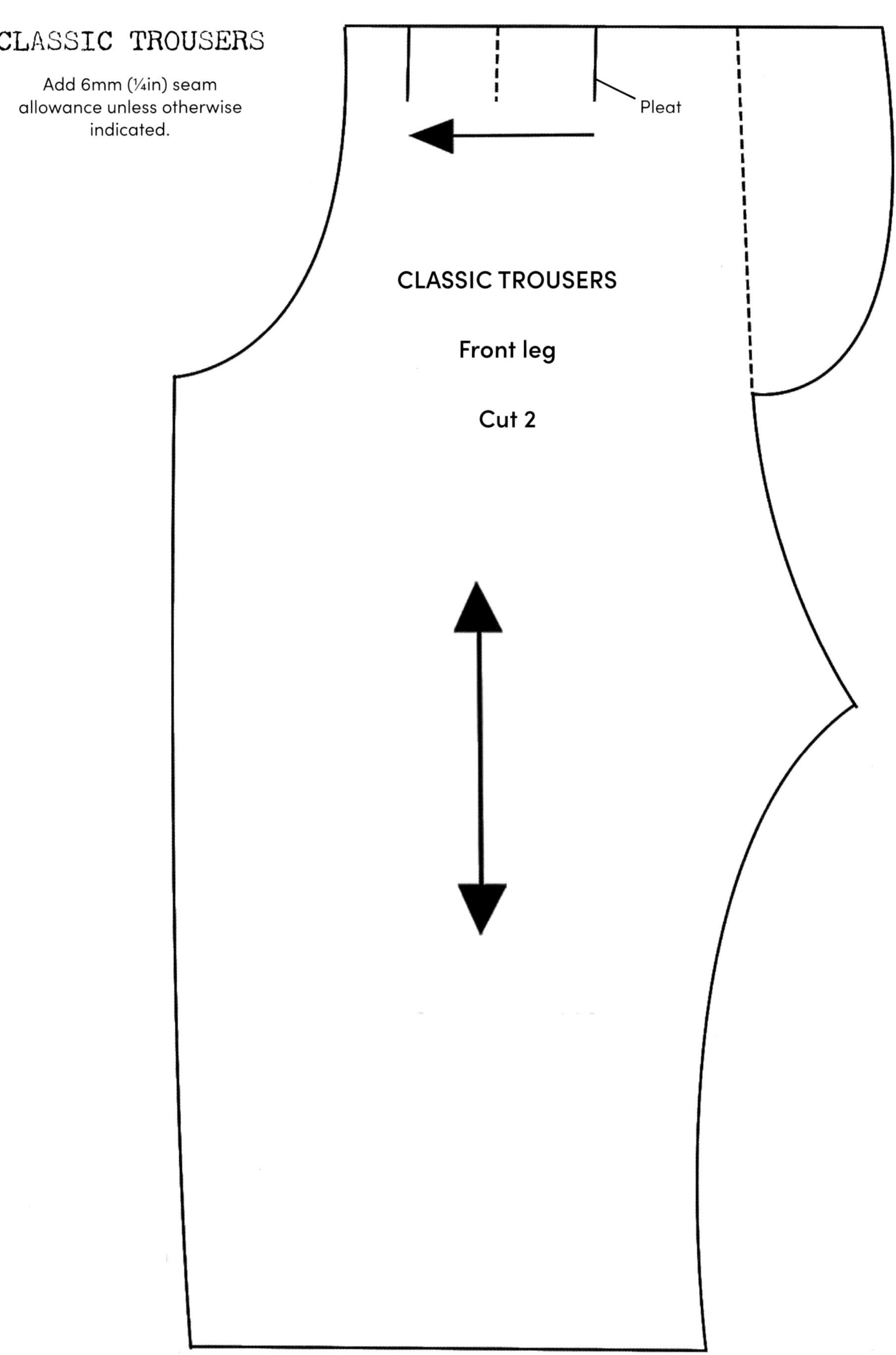

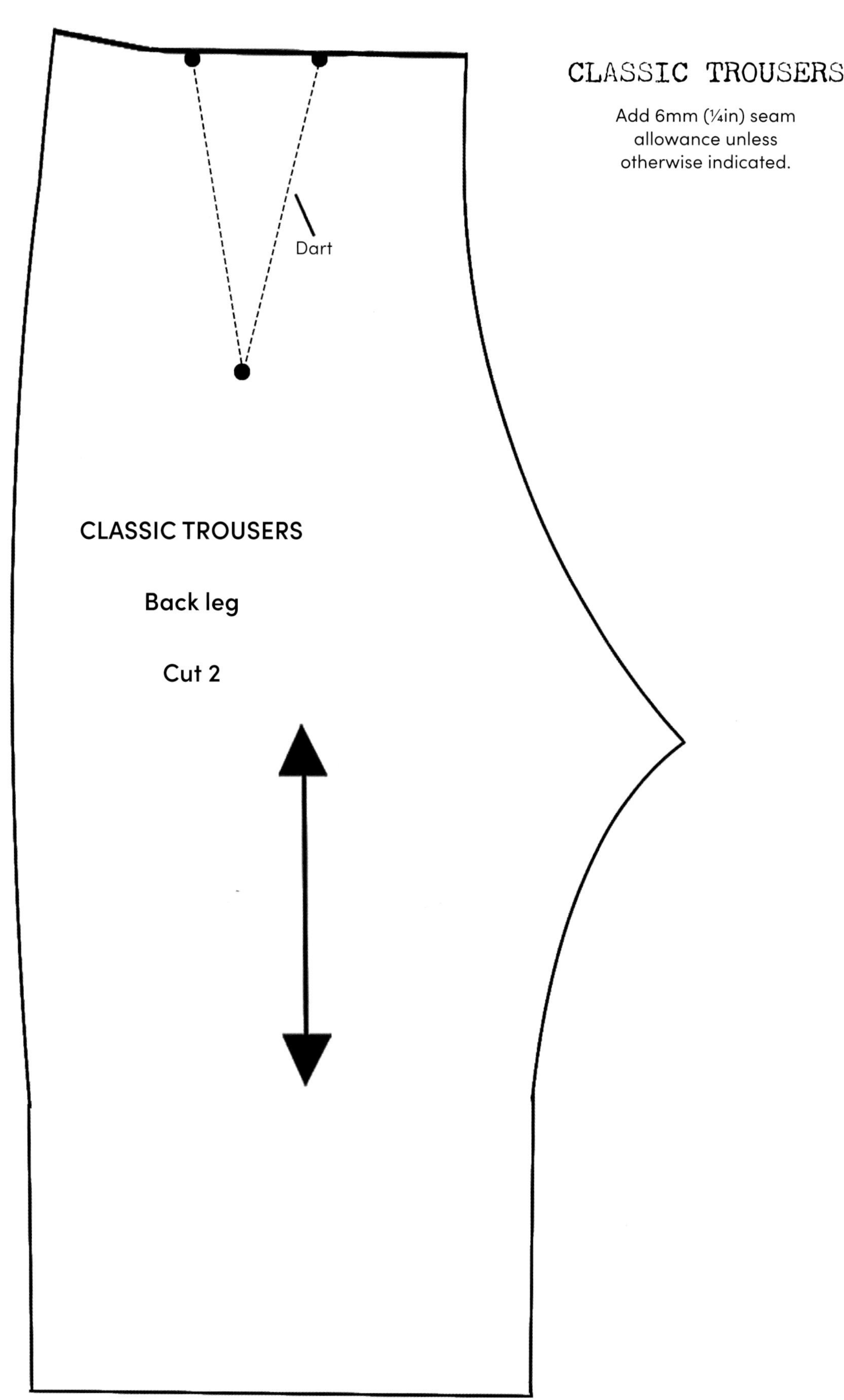

CLASSIC TROUSERS

Add 6mm (¼in) seam allowance unless otherwise indicated.

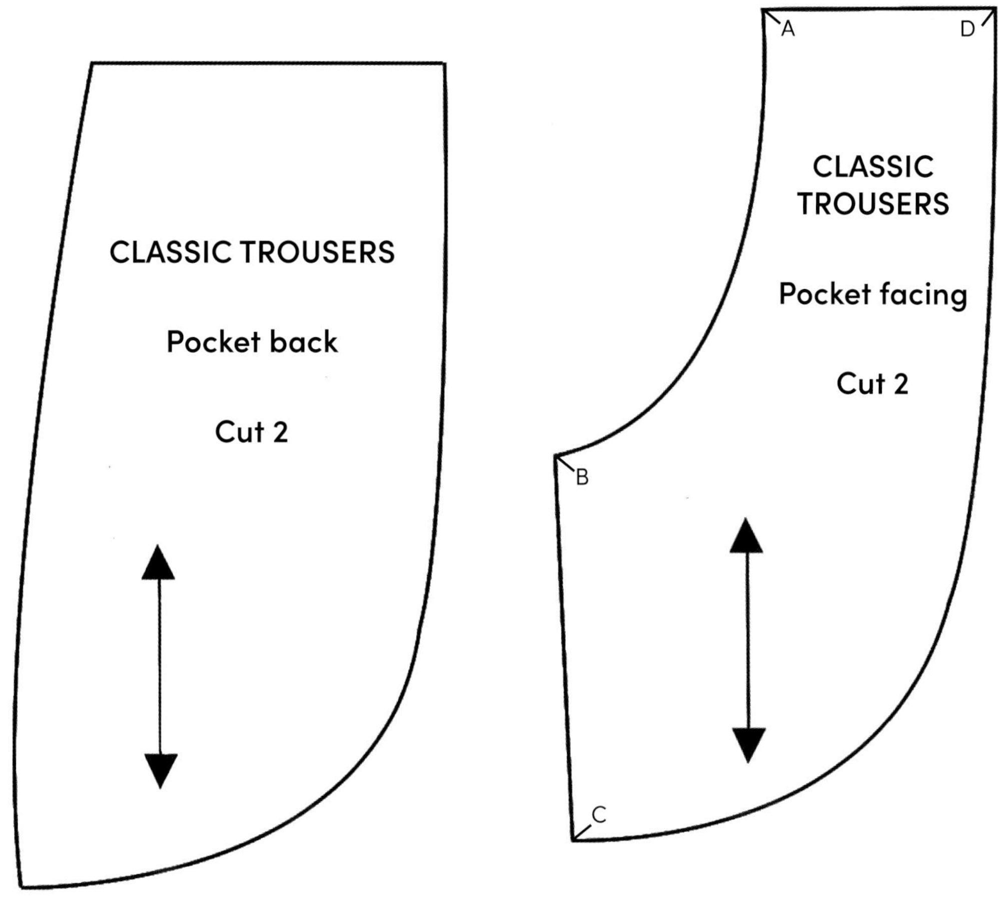
CLASSIC TROUSERS
Pocket back
Cut 2
A
D
CLASSIC TROUSERS
Pocket facing
Cut 2
B
C

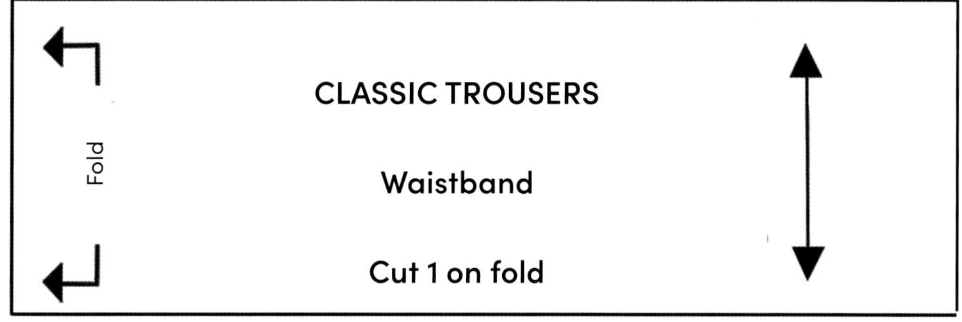
CLASSIC TROUSERS
Waistband
Cut 1 on fold
Fold

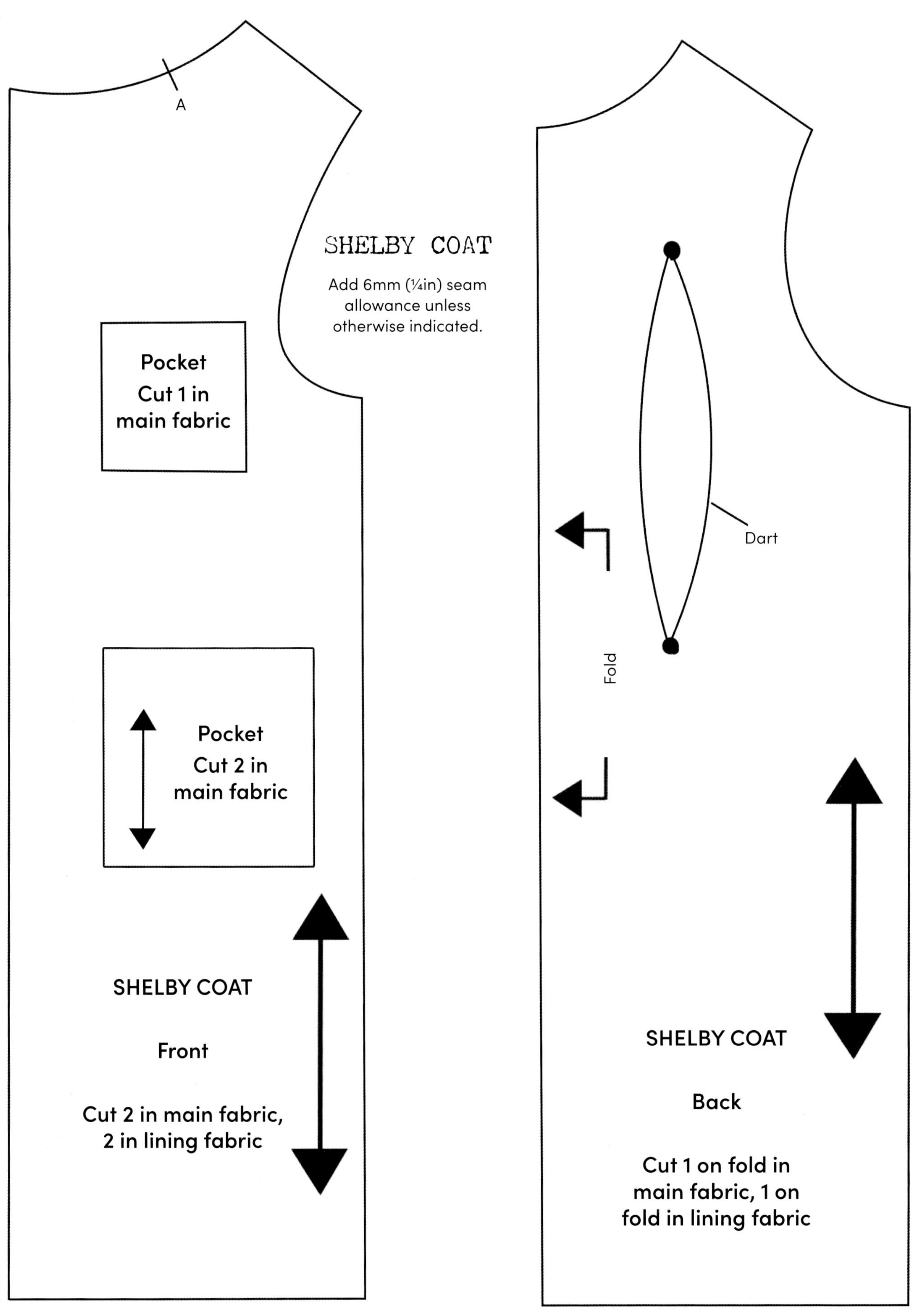
A
SHELBY COAT
Add 6mm (¼in) seam allowance unless otherwise indicated.
Pocket
Cut 1 in main fabric
Pocket
Cut 2 in main fabric
SHELBY COAT
Front
Cut 2 in main fabric, 2 in lining fabric
Dart
Fold
SHELBY COAT
Back
Cut 1 on fold in main fabric, 1 on fold in lining fabric

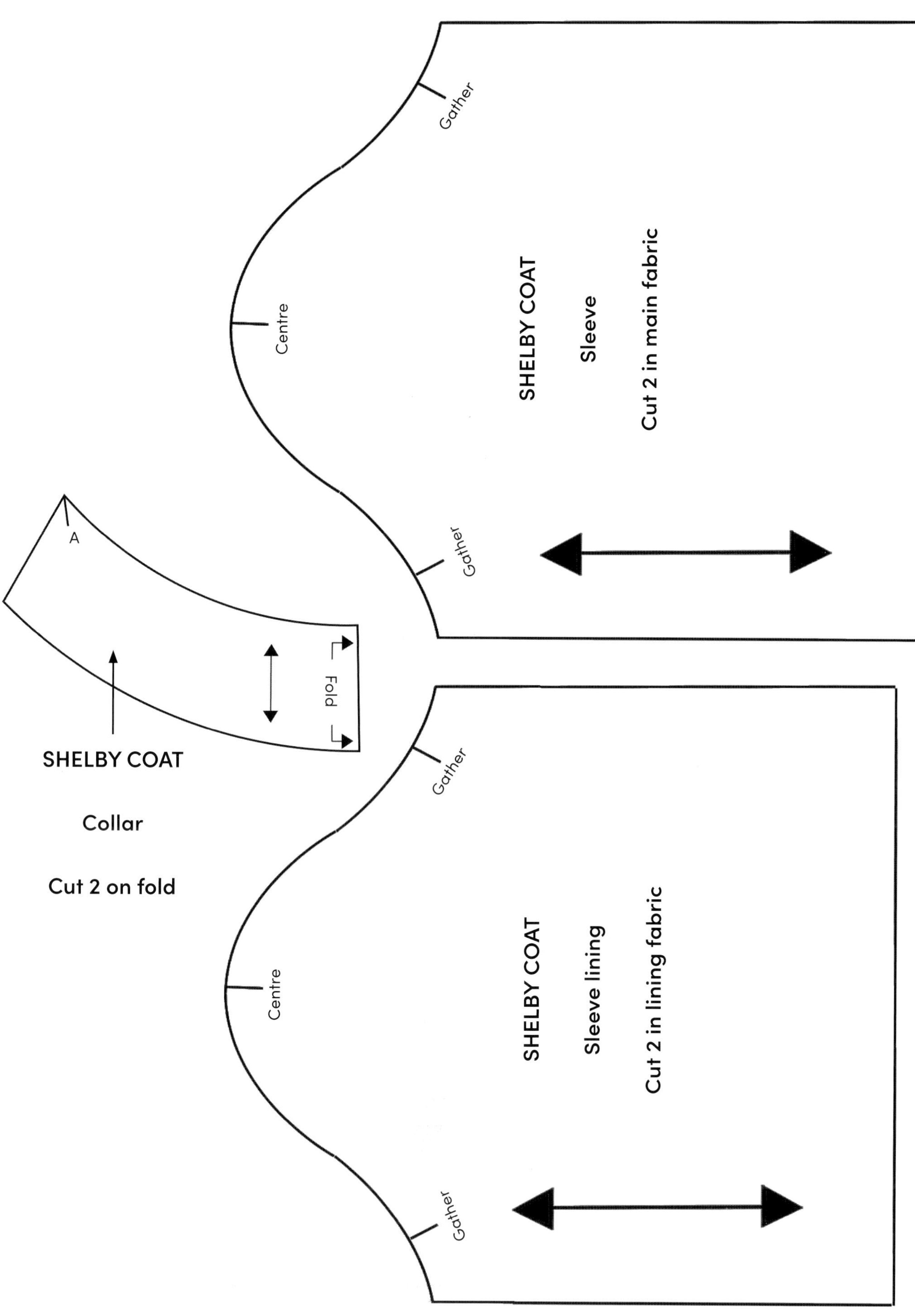
SHELBY COAT
Sleeve
Cut 2 in main fabric
Gather
Centre
Gather
A
Fold
SHELBY COAT
Collar
Cut 2 on fold
SHELBY COAT
Sleeve lining
Cut 2 in lining fabric
Gather
Centre
Gather

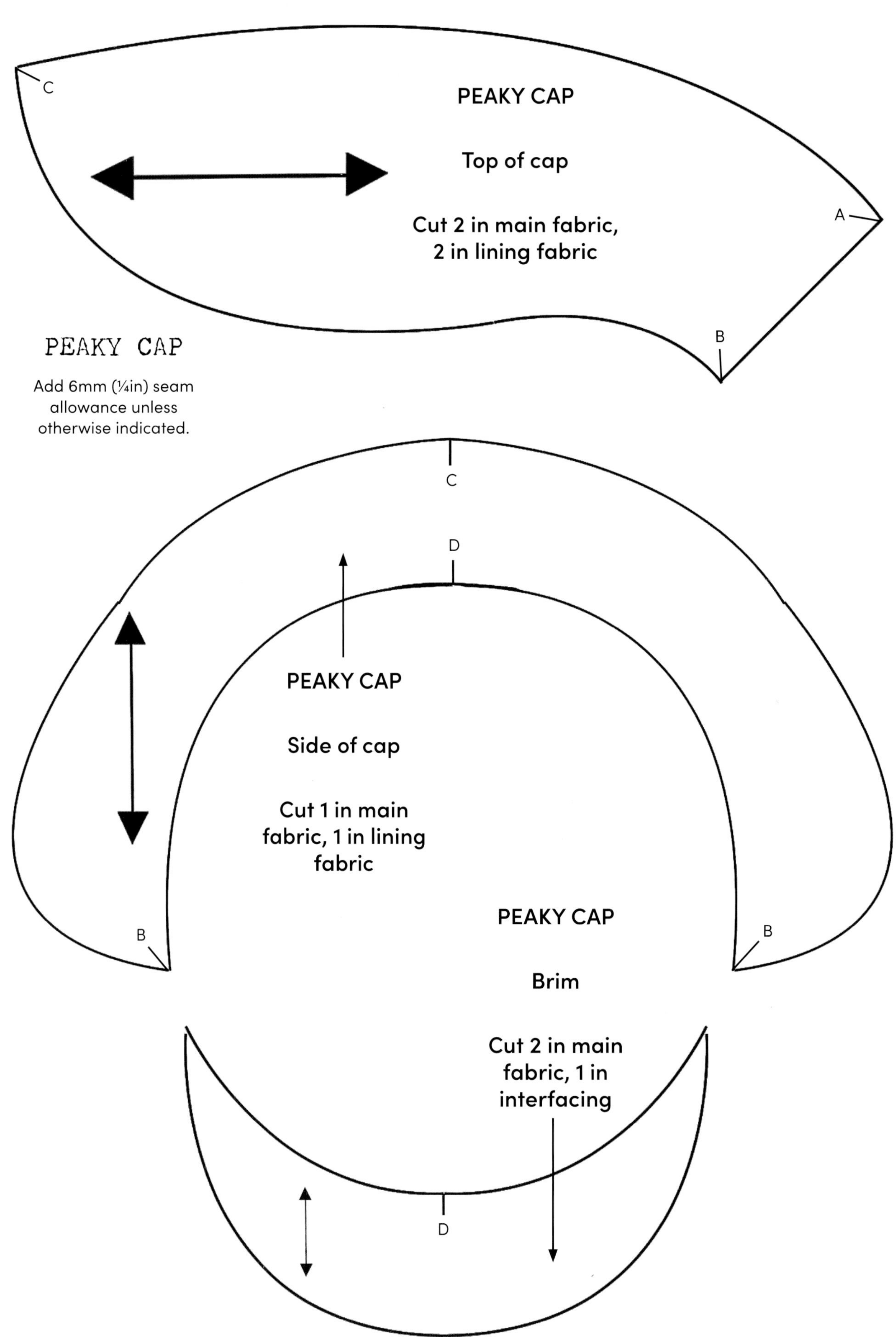
C
PEAKY CAP
Top of cap
Cut 2 in main fabric,
2 in lining fabric
A
B
PEAKY CAP
Add 6mm (¼in) seam
allowance unless
otherwise indicated.
C
D
PEAKY CAP
Side of cap
Cut 1 in main
fabric, 1 in lining
fabric
B
B
PEAKY CAP
Brim
Cut 2 in main
fabric, 1 in
interfacing
D

HORSESHOE WAISTCOAT

Add 6mm (¼in) seam allowance unless otherwise indicated.

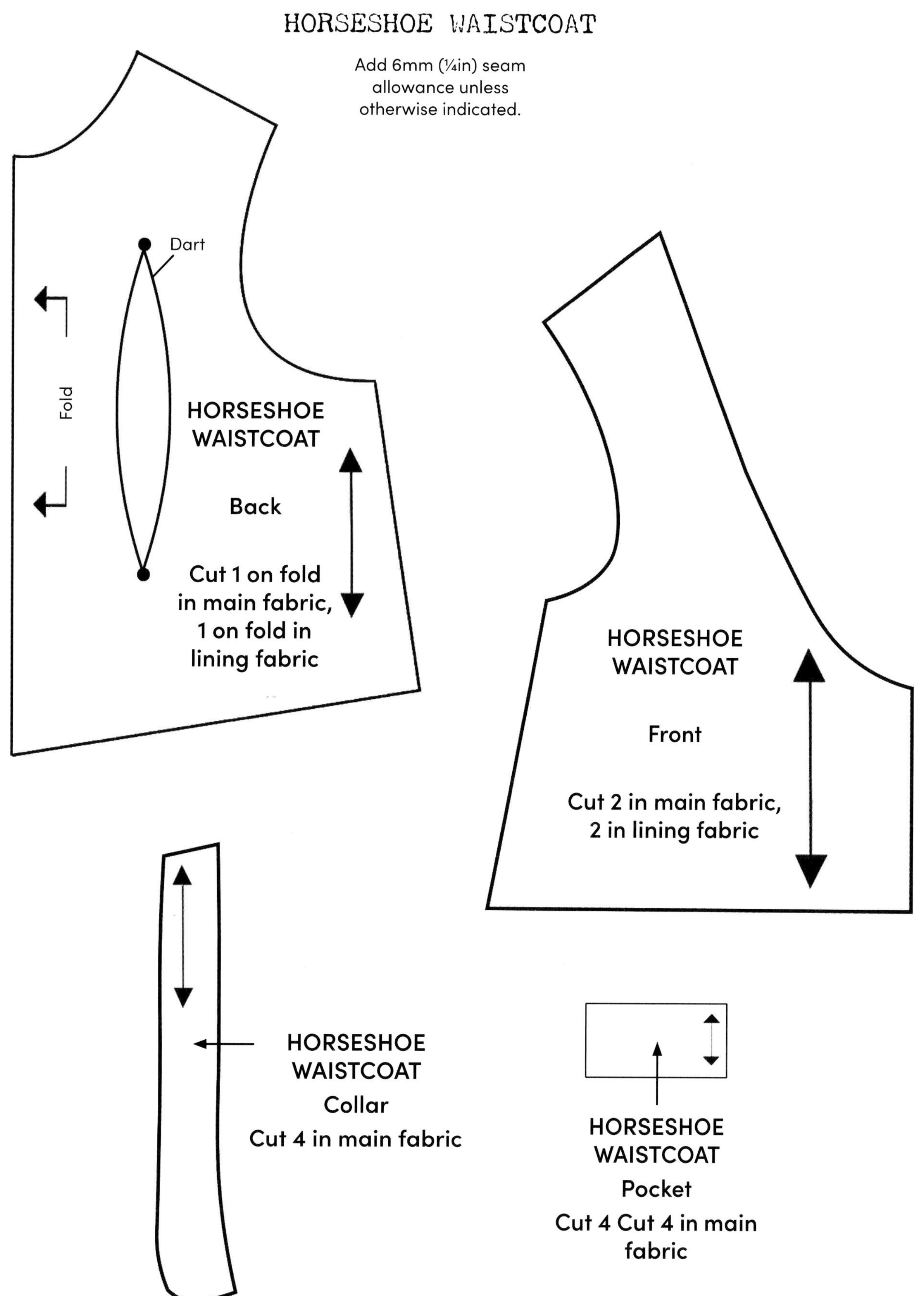

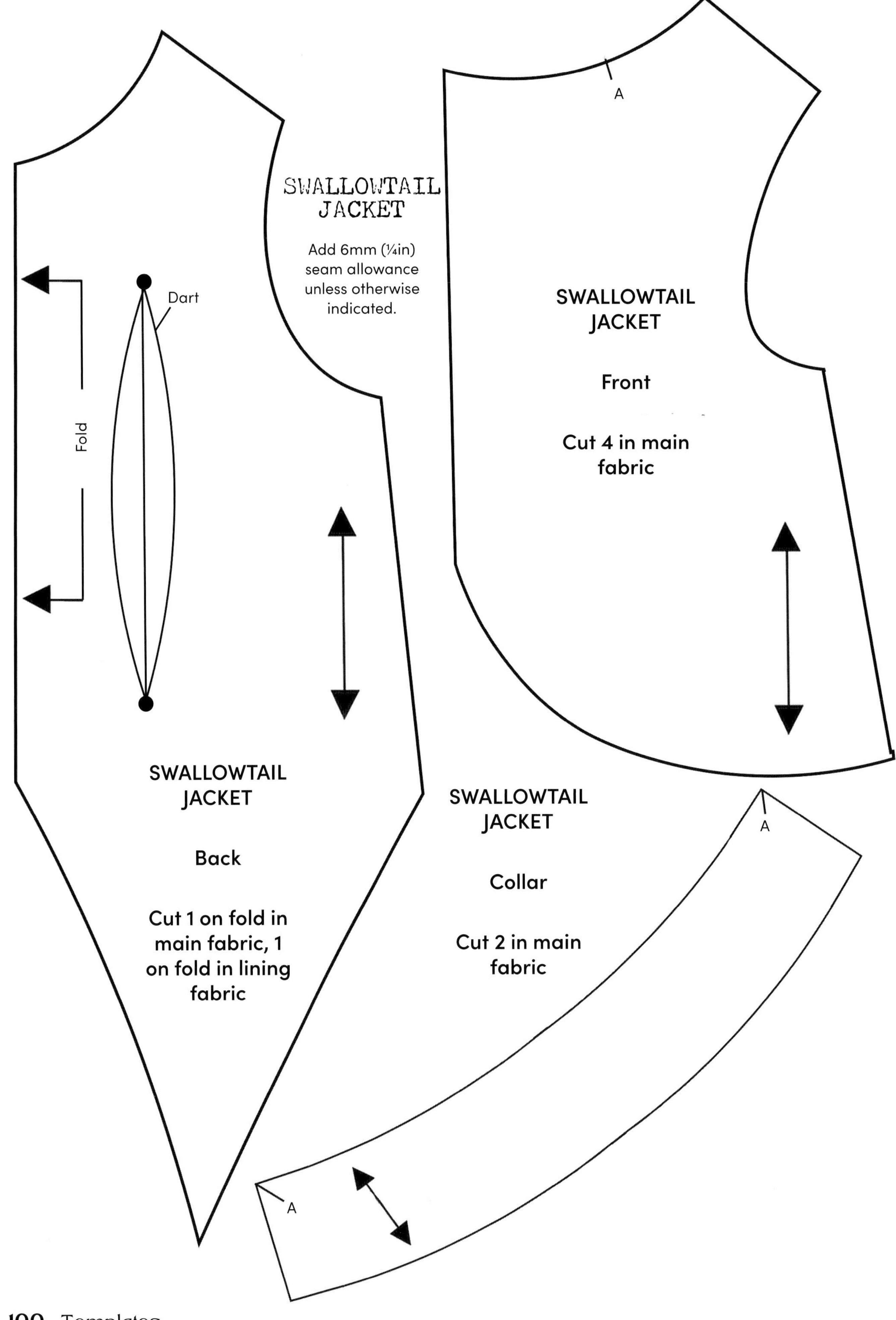
SWALLOWTAIL
JACKET
Add 6mm (¼in) seam allowance unless otherwise indicated.
Dart
Fold
SWALLOWTAIL
JACKET
Back
Cut 1 on fold in main fabric, 1 on fold in lining fabric
A
SWALLOWTAIL
JACKET
Front
Cut 4 in main fabric
SWALLOWTAIL
JACKET
Collar
Cut 2 in main fabric
A
A

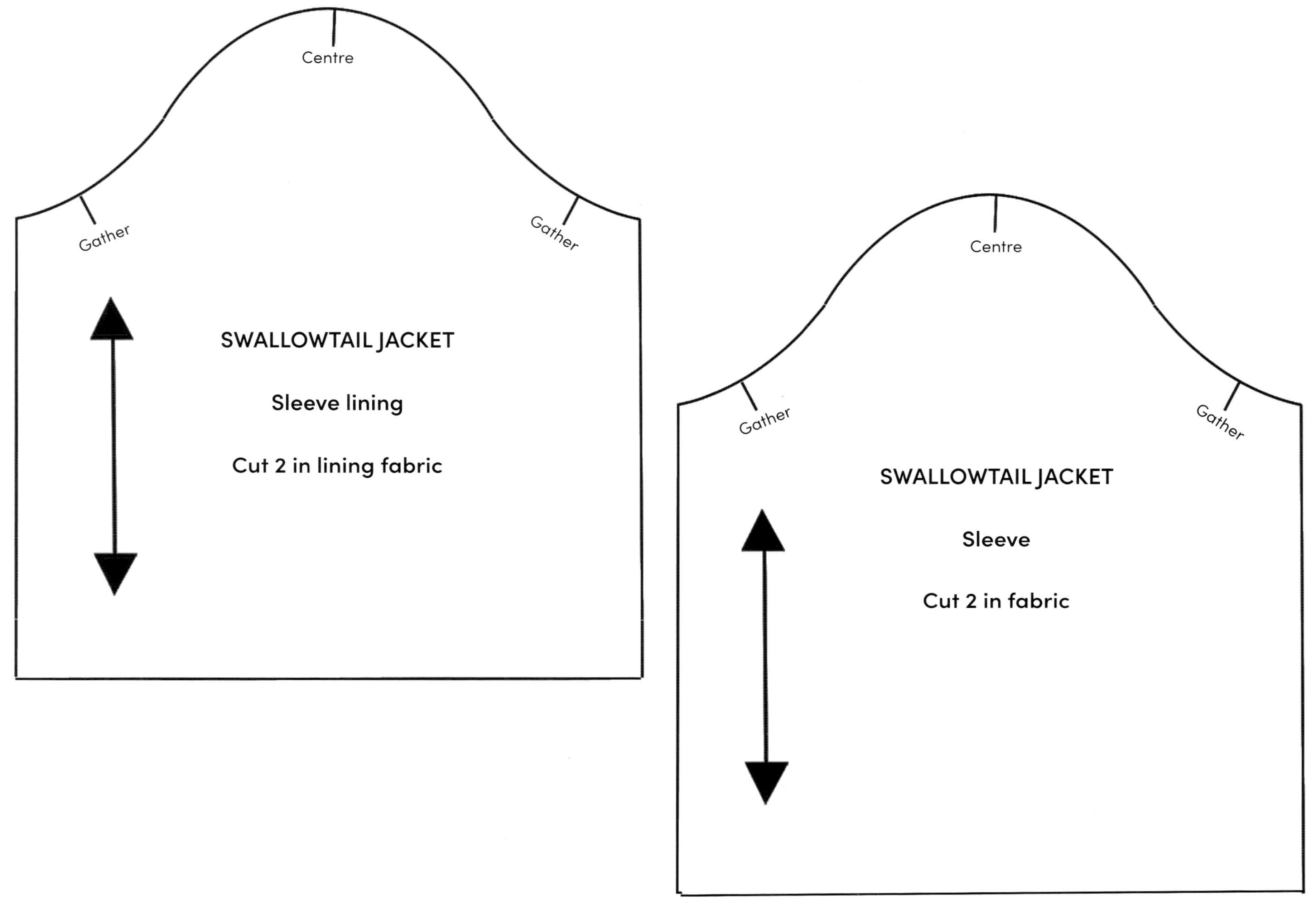
Centre
Gather
Gather
SWALLOWTAIL JACKET
Sleeve lining
Cut 2 in lining fabric
Centre
Gather
Gather
SWALLOWTAIL JACKET
Sleeve
Cut 2 in fabric

Add 6mm (¼in) seam allowance unless otherwise indicated.

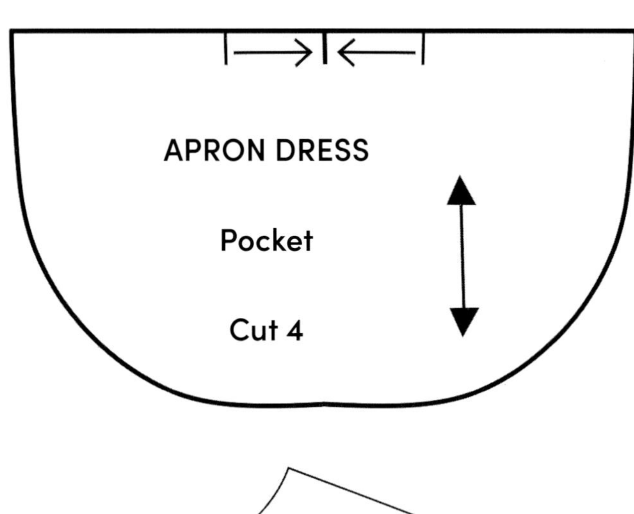

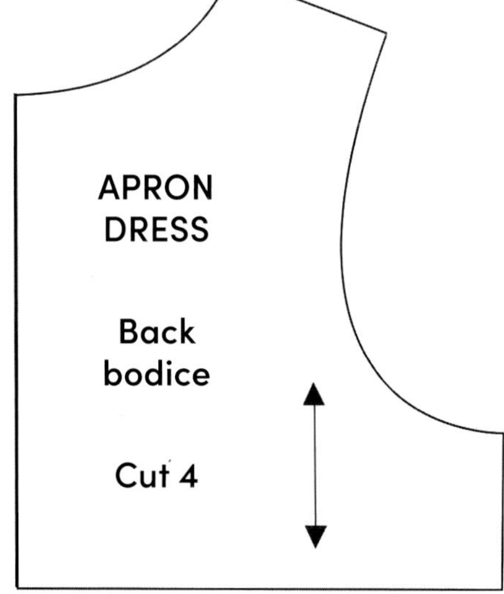

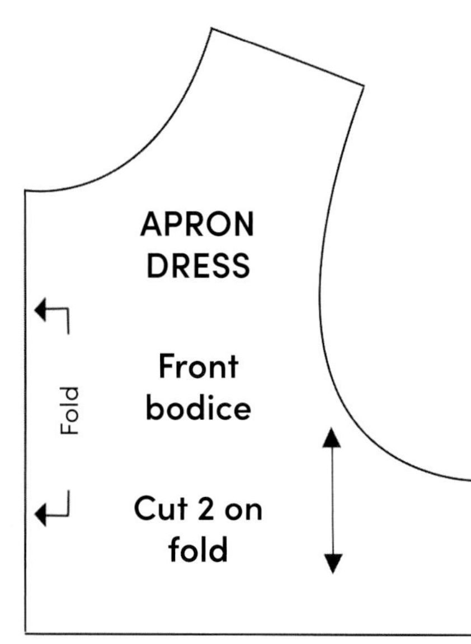

APRON DRESS WITH APPLIQUÉ

Do not add seam allowance to appliqué templates

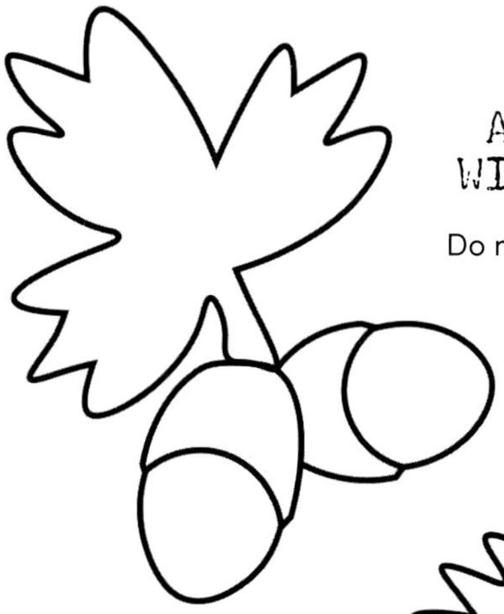

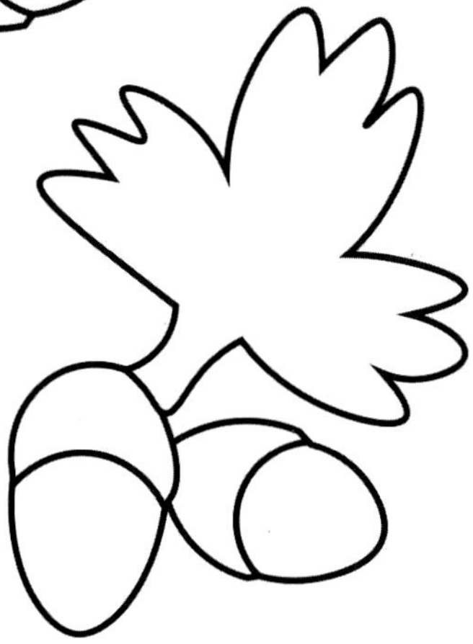

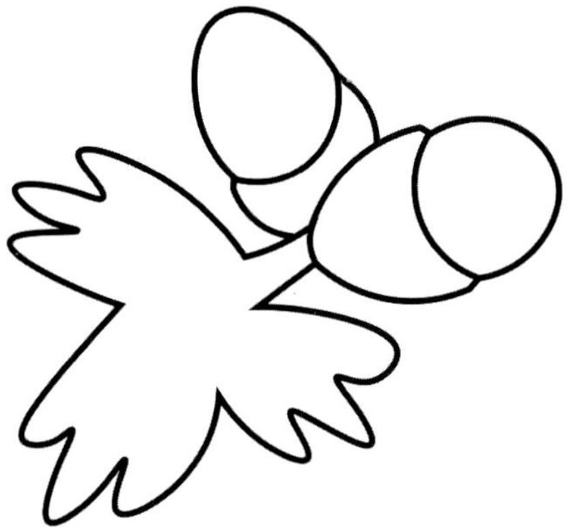

APRON DRESS

Acorn appliqué motifs

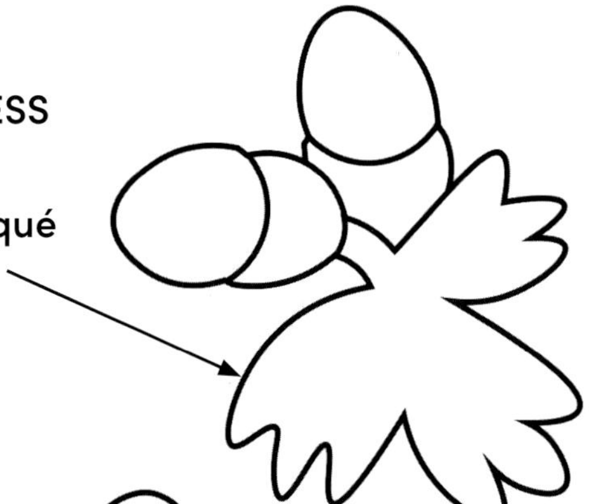

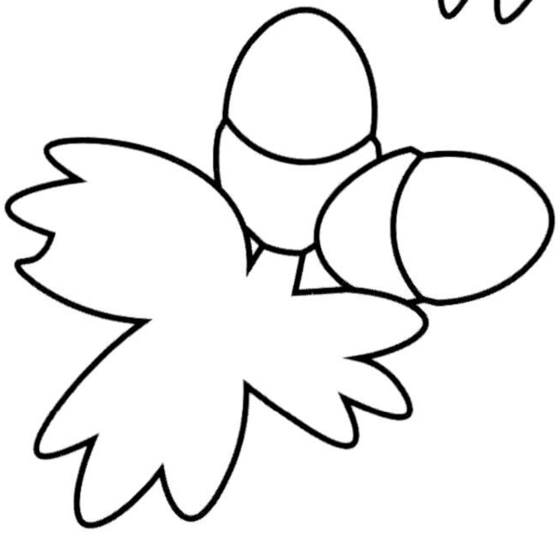

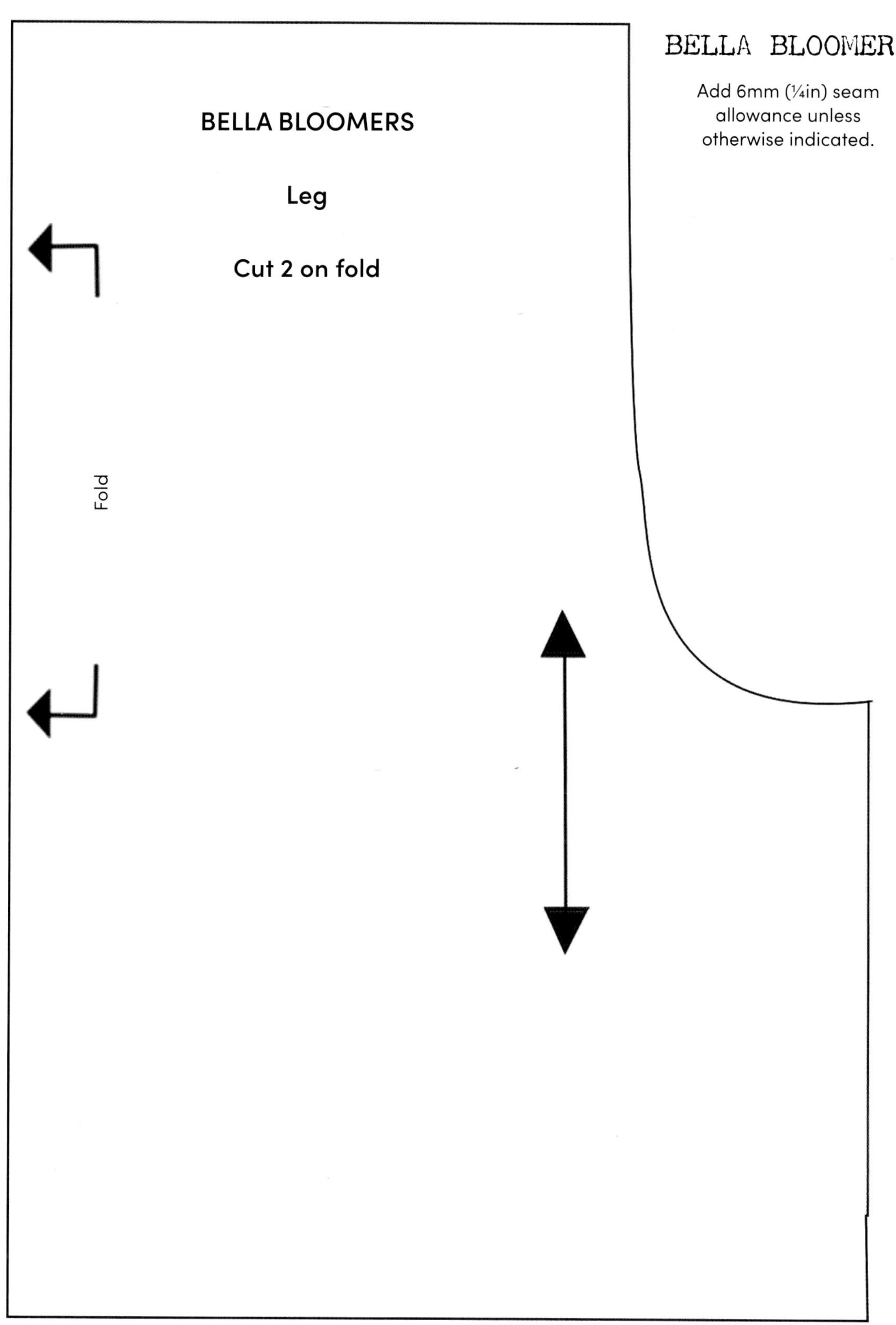

BELLA BLOOMERS

Add 6mm (¼in) seam allowance unless otherwise indicated.

JOSEPHINE JACKET

Add 6mm (¼in) seam allowance unless otherwise indicated.

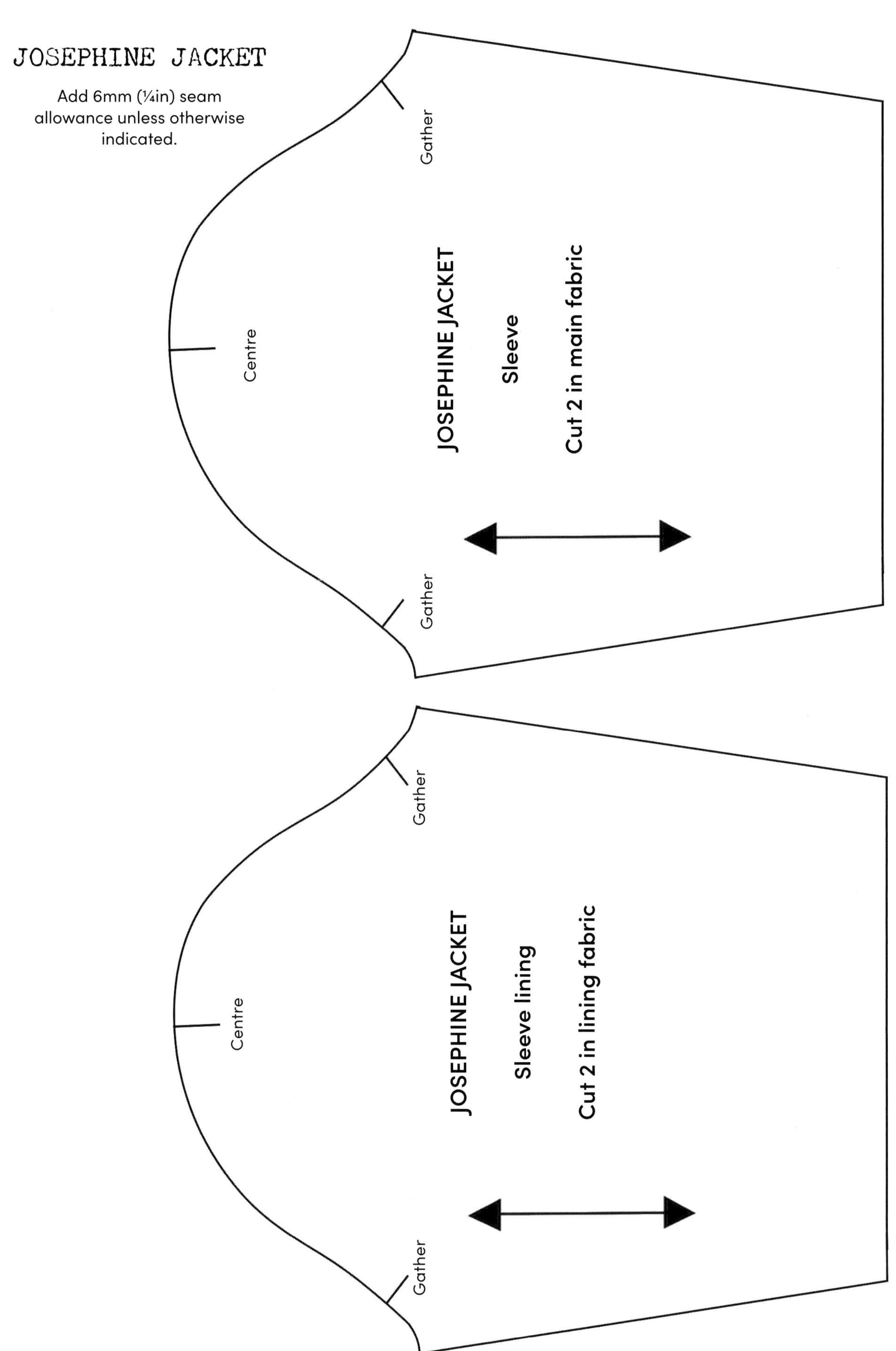

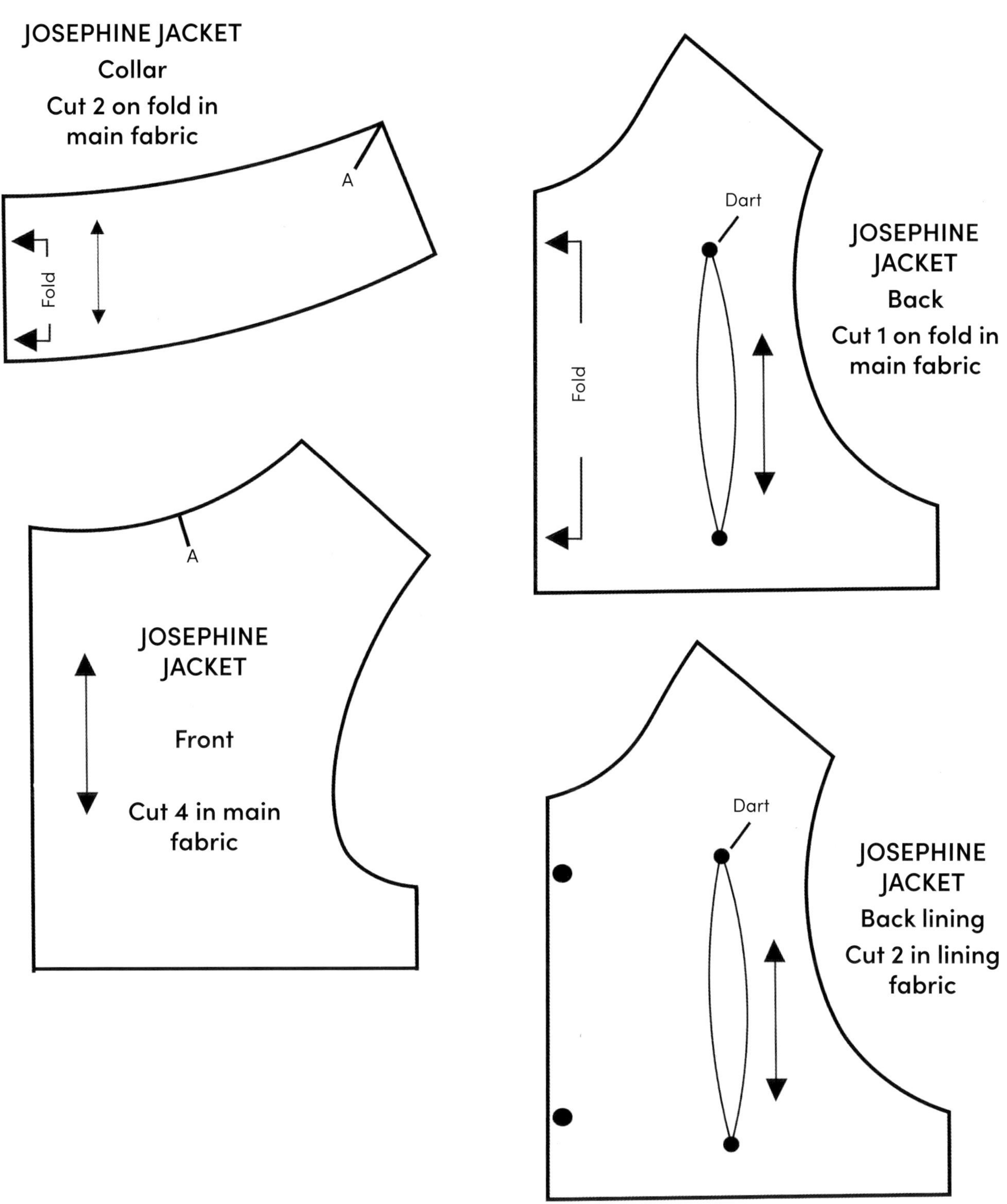
JOSEPHINE JACKET
Collar
Cut 2 on fold in main fabric
A
Fold
JOSEPHINE JACKET
Back
Cut 1 on fold in main fabric
Dart
Fold
A
JOSEPHINE JACKET
Front
Cut 4 in main fabric
JOSEPHINE JACKET
Back lining
Cut 2 in lining fabric
Dart

HARRIS JACKET

Add 6mm (¼in) seam allowance unless otherwise indicated.

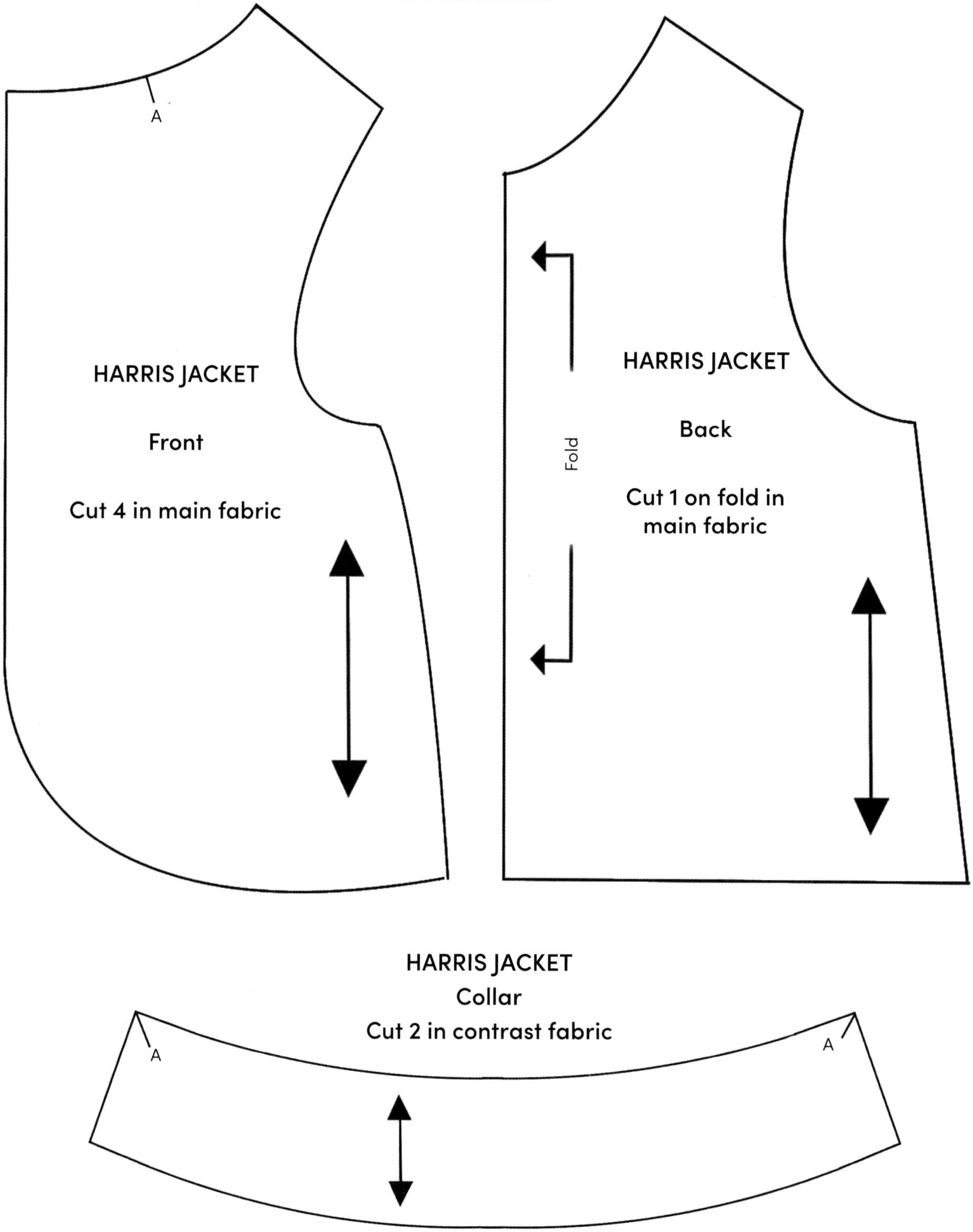

A

HARRIS JACKET

Front

Cut 4 in main fabric

Fold

HARRIS JACKET

Back

Cut 1 on fold in main fabric

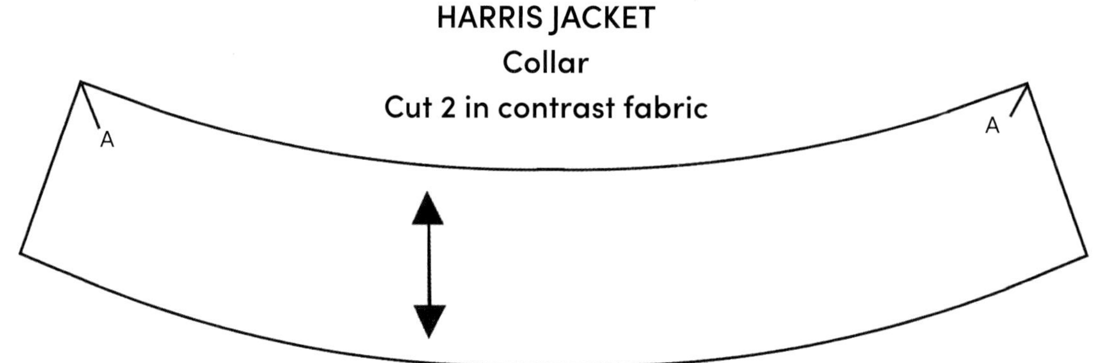

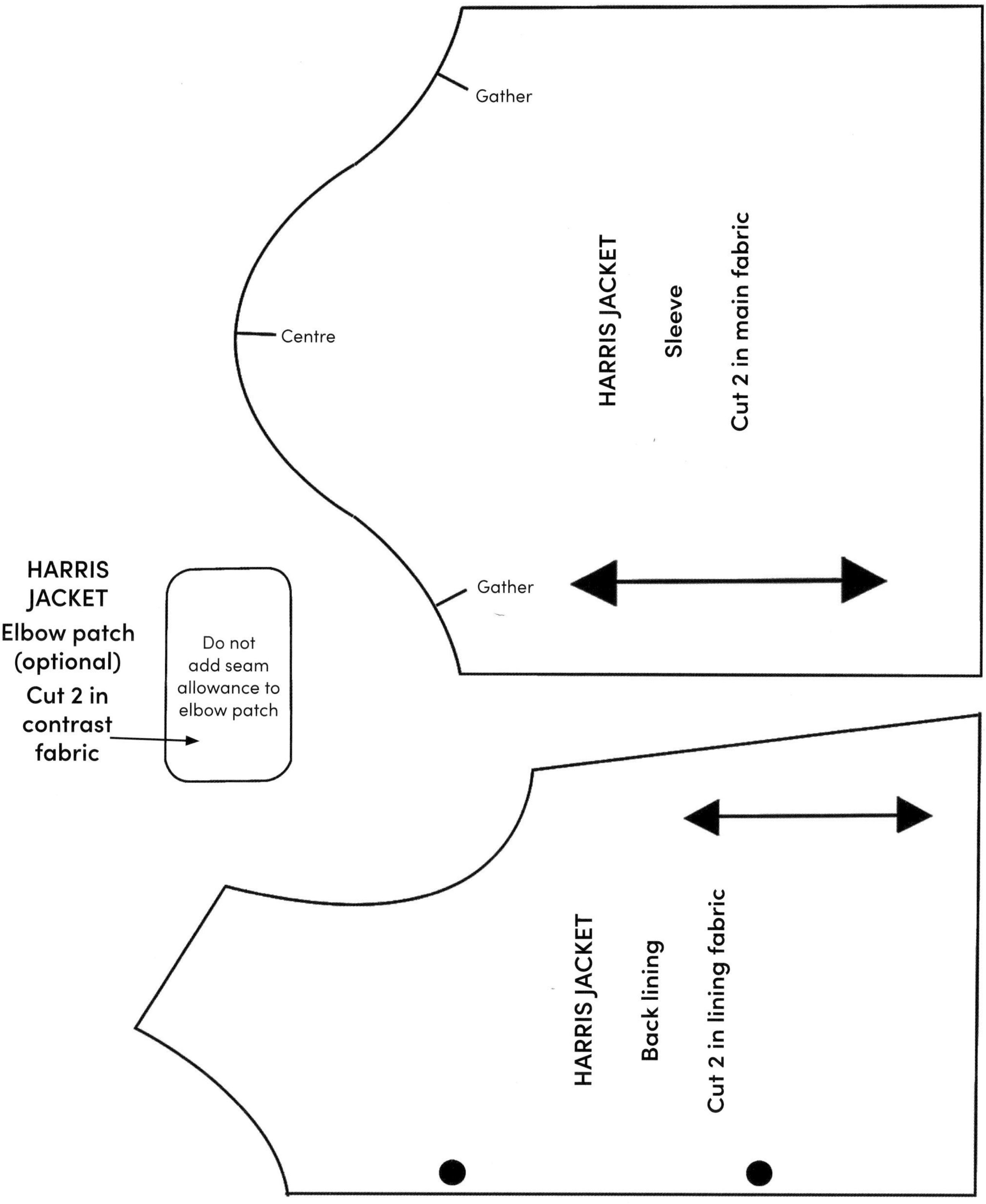
Gather
Centre
Gather
HARRIS JACKET
Sleeve
Cut 2 in main fabric
HARRIS JACKET
Elbow patch (optional)
Cut 2 in contrast fabric
Do not add seam allowance to elbow patch
HARRIS JACKET
Back lining
Cut 2 in lining fabric

HARRIS JACKET

Add 6mm (¼in) seam allowance unless otherwise indicated.

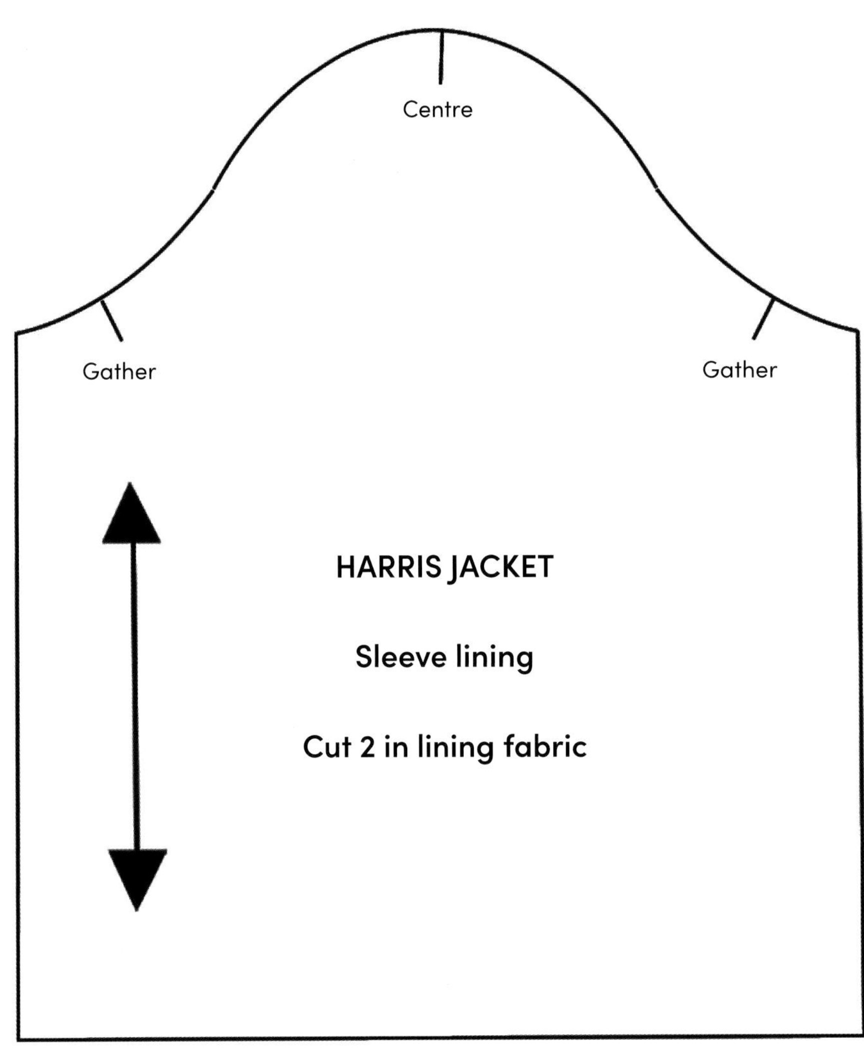

BERRY BRIM HAT

Add 6mm (¼in) seam allowance unless otherwise indicated.

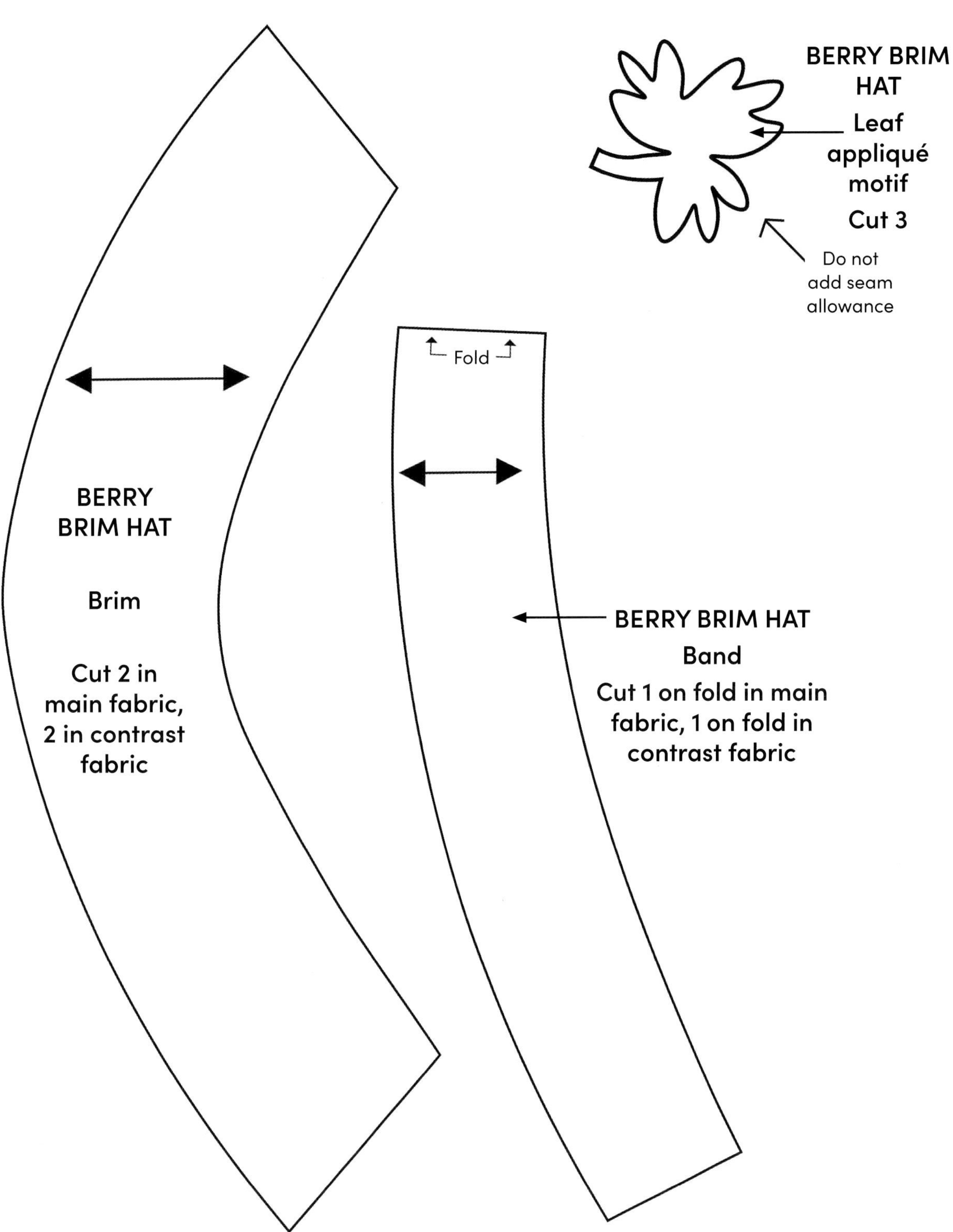

PERFECT PETAL JACKET

Add 6mm (¼in) seam allowance unless otherwise indicated.

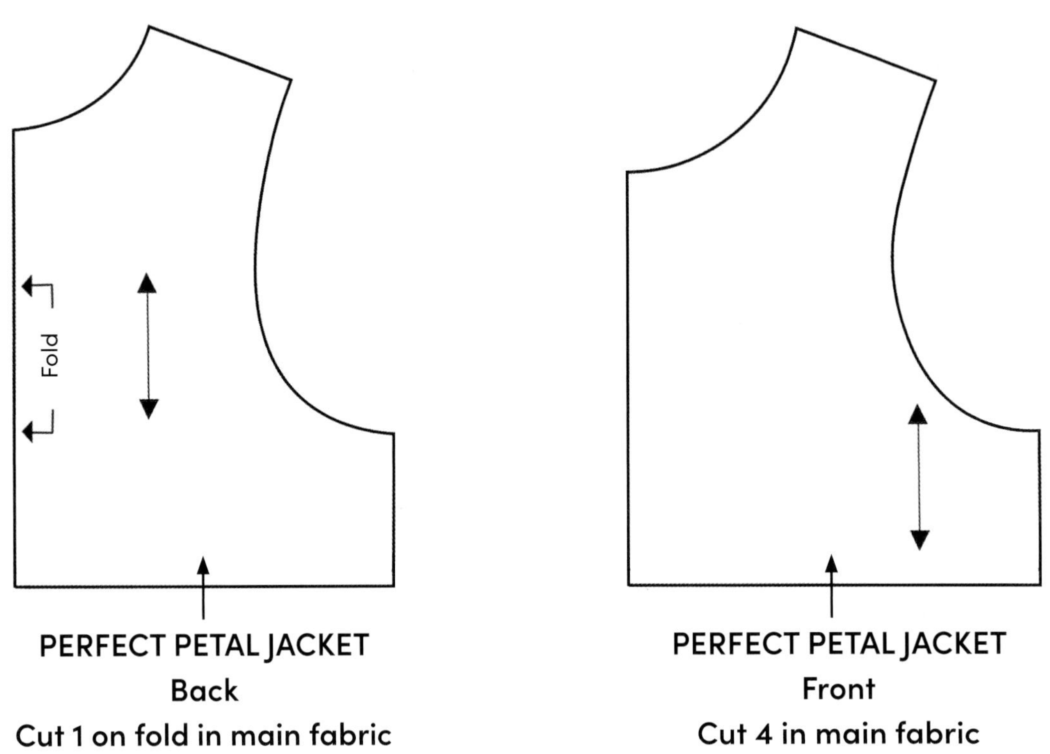

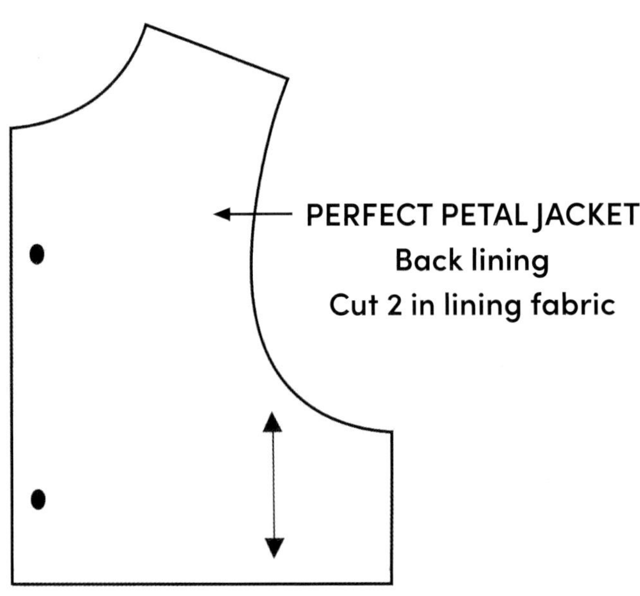

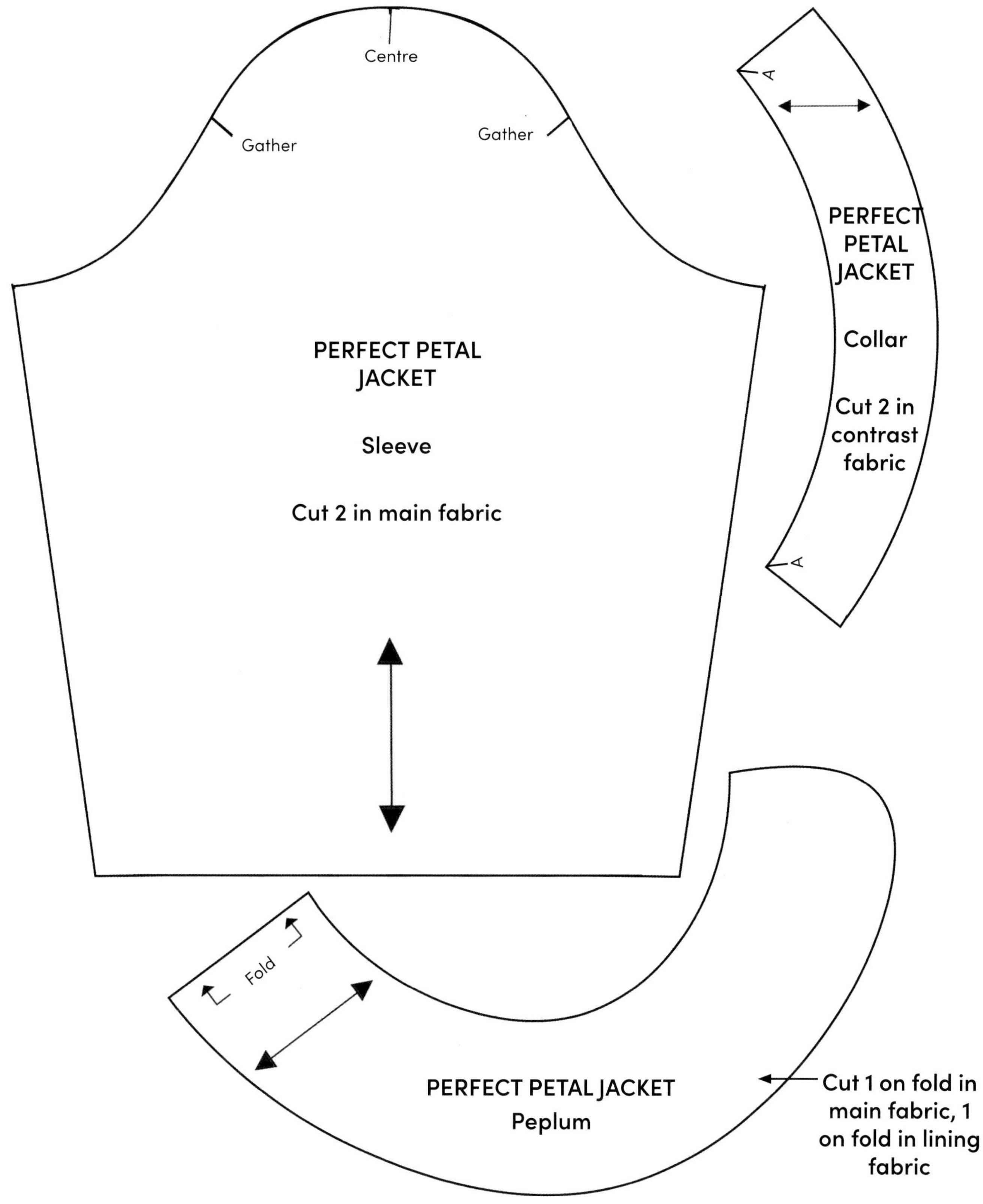
Centre
Gather
Gather
PERFECT PETAL JACKET
Sleeve
Cut 2 in main fabric
A
PERFECT PETAL JACKET
Collar
Cut 2 in contrast fabric
A
Fold
PERFECT PETAL JACKET
Peplum
Cut 1 on fold in main fabric, 1 on fold in lining fabric

PERFECT PETAL JACKET

Add 6mm (¼in) seam allowance unless otherwise indicated.

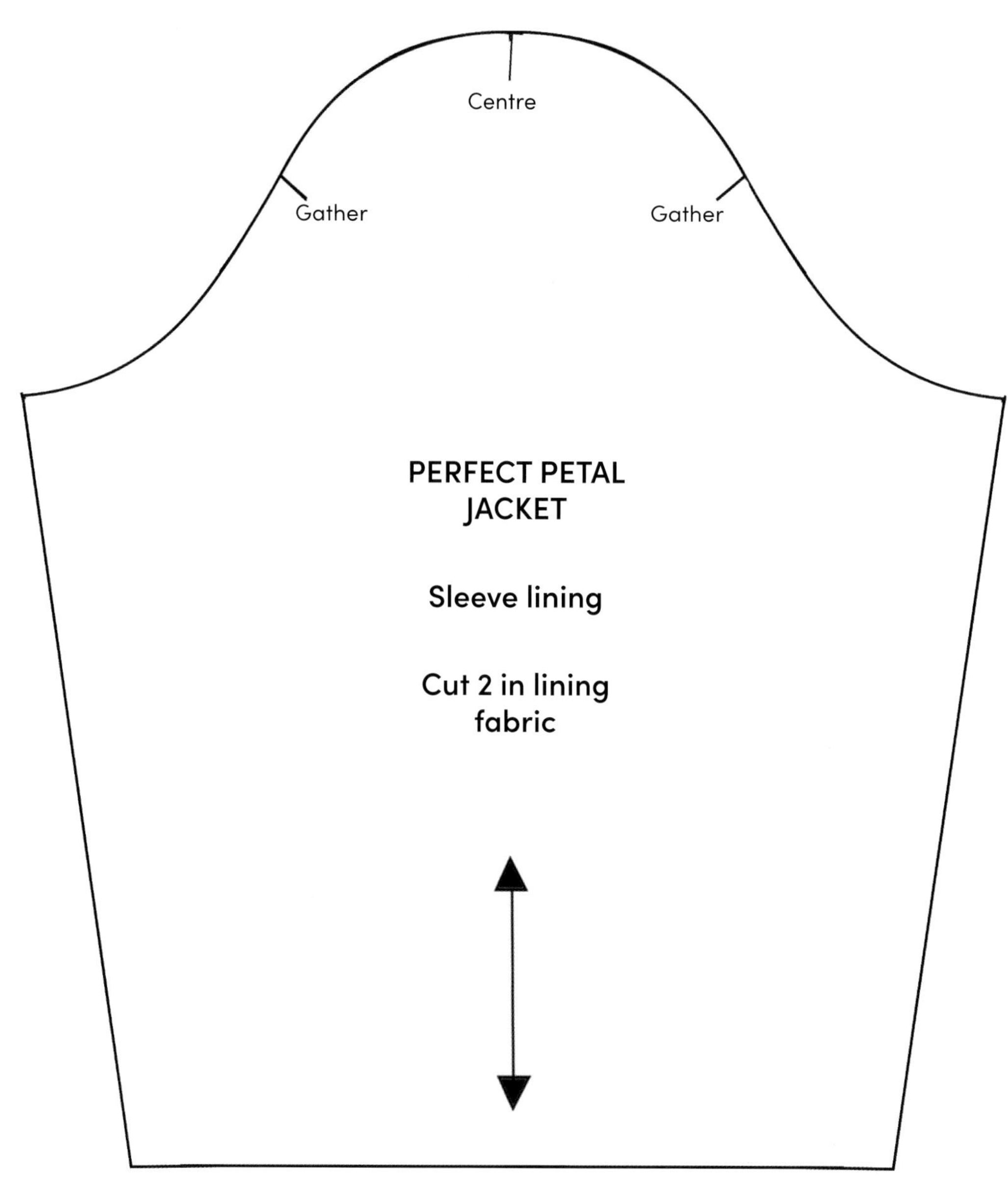

MANDARIN WAISTCOAT

Add 6mm (¼in) seam allowance unless otherwise indicated.

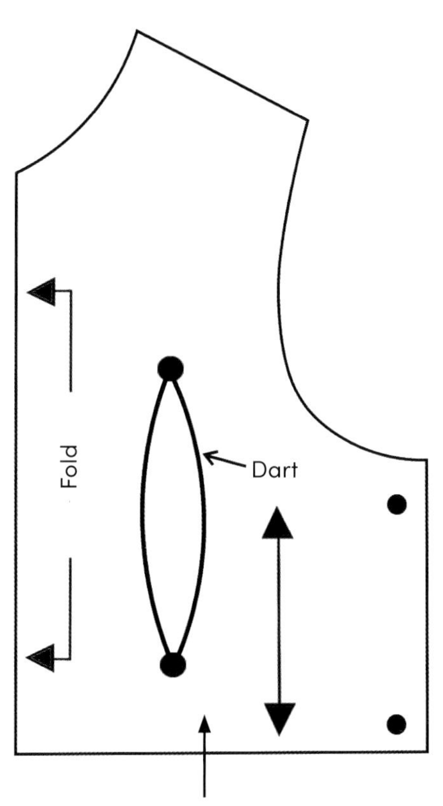

MANDARIN WAISTCOAT
Back
Cut 1 on fold in main fabric, 1 on fold in lining fabric

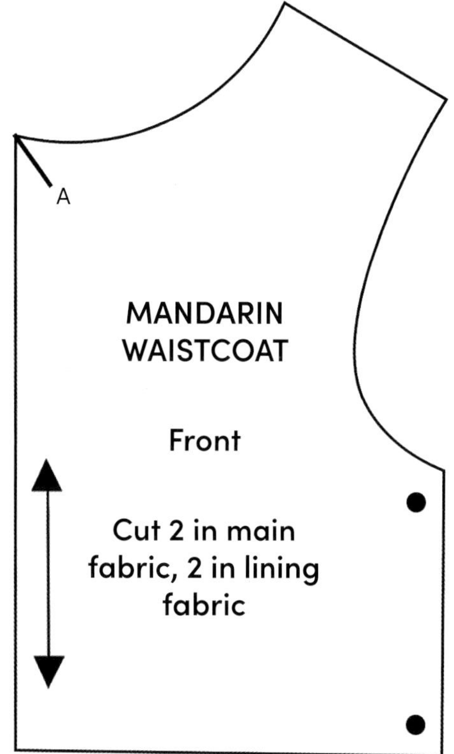

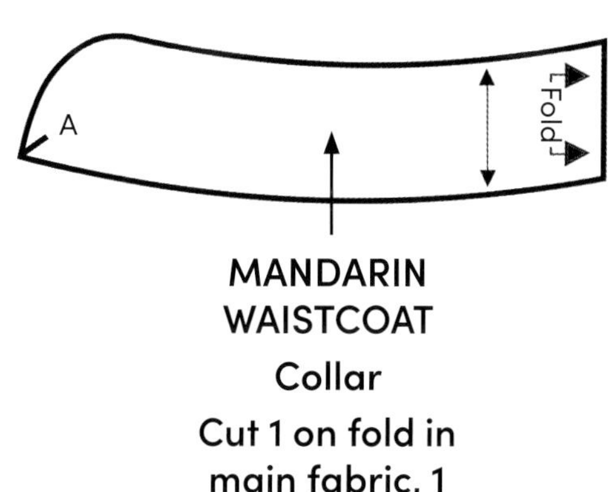

MANDARIN WAISTCOAT
Collar
Cut 1 on fold in main fabric, 1 on fold in lining fabric

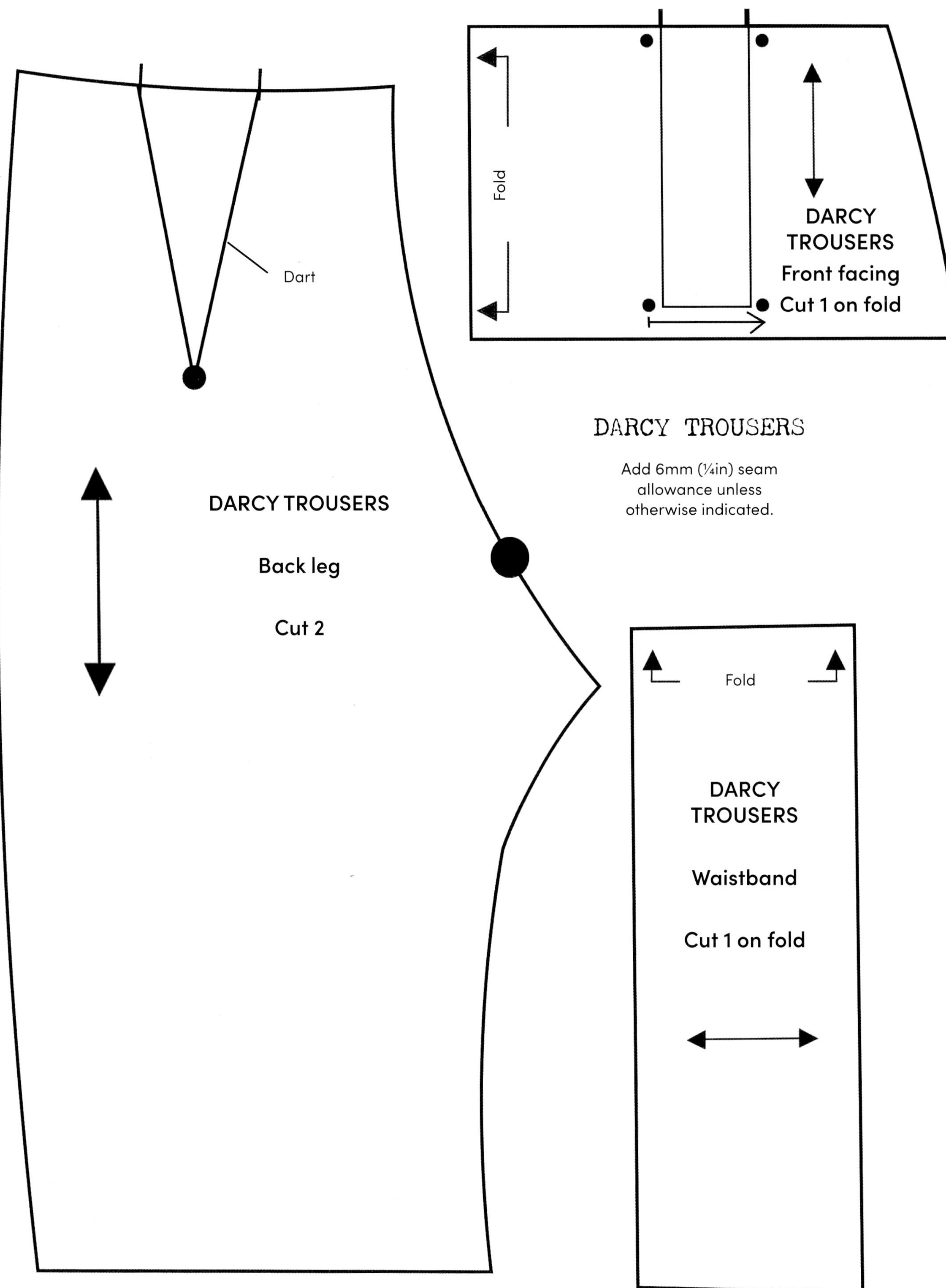
Fold
DARCY TROUSERS
Front facing
Cut 1 on fold
Dart
DARCY TROUSERS
Back leg
Cut 2
DARCY TROUSERS
Add 6mm (¼in) seam allowance unless otherwise indicated.
Fold
DARCY TROUSERS
Waistband
Cut 1 on fold

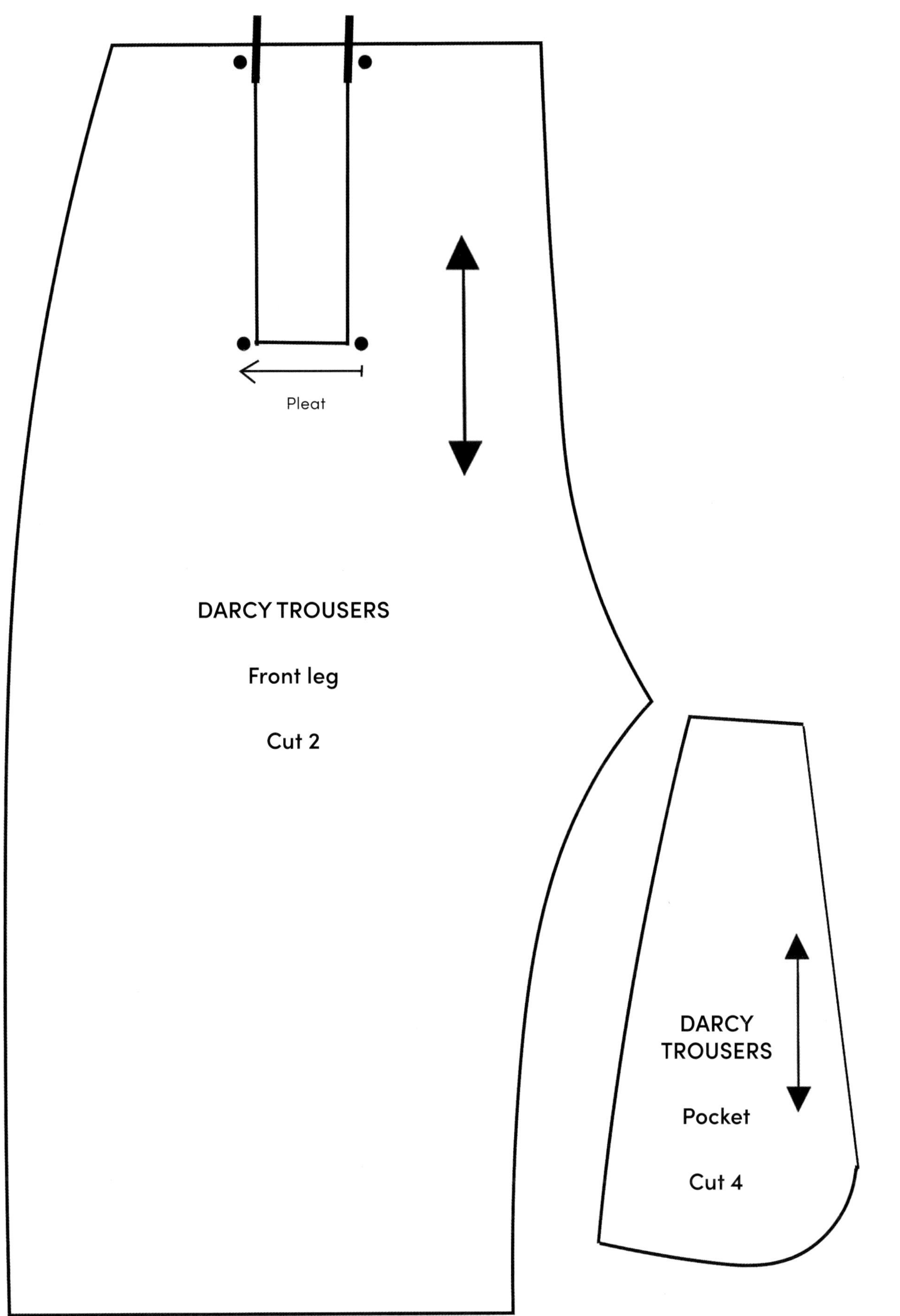
Pleat
DARCY TROUSERS
Front leg
Cut 2
DARCY TROUSERS
Pocket
Cut 4

REGENCY JACKET

Add 6mm (¼in) seam allowance unless otherwise indicated.

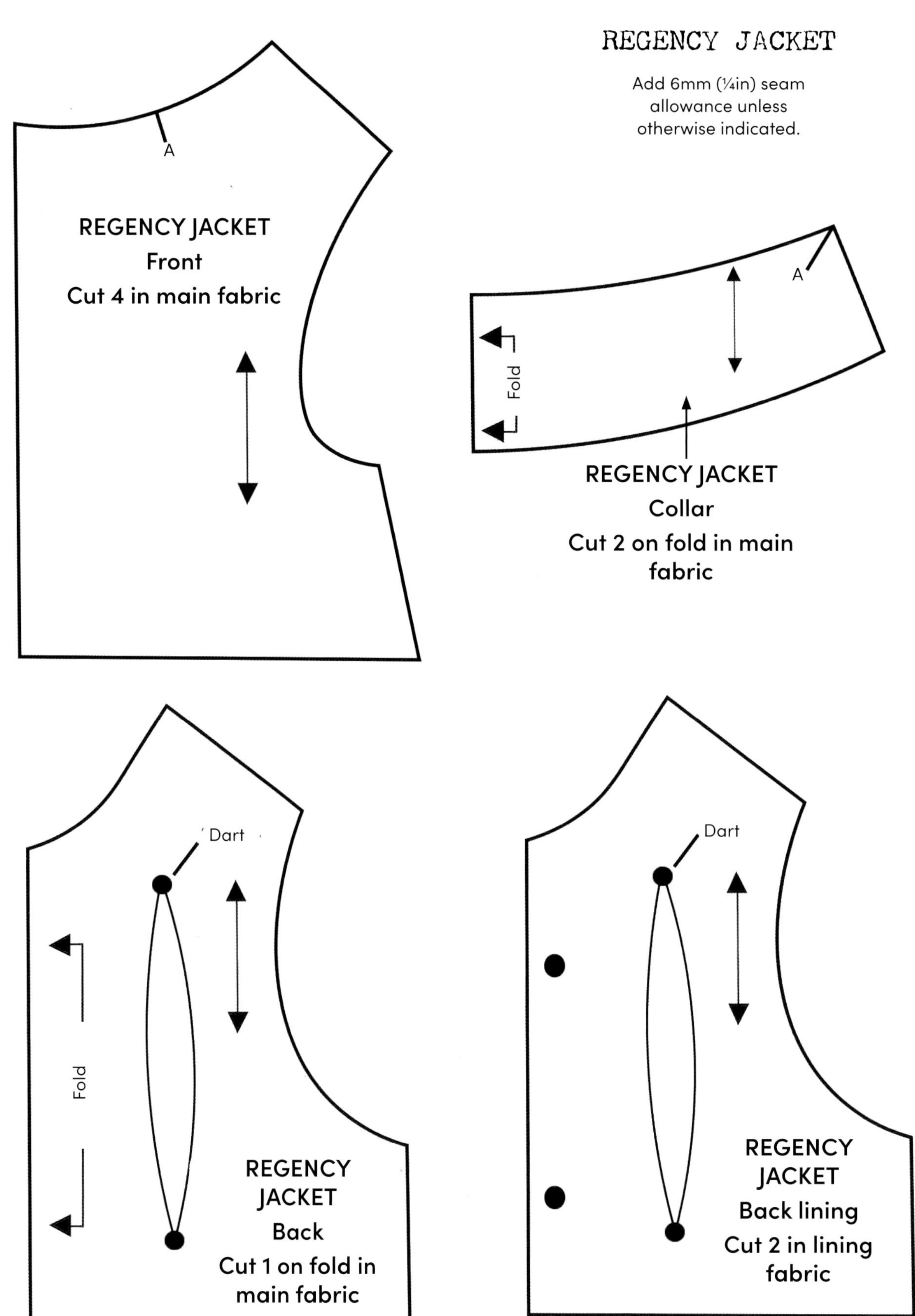

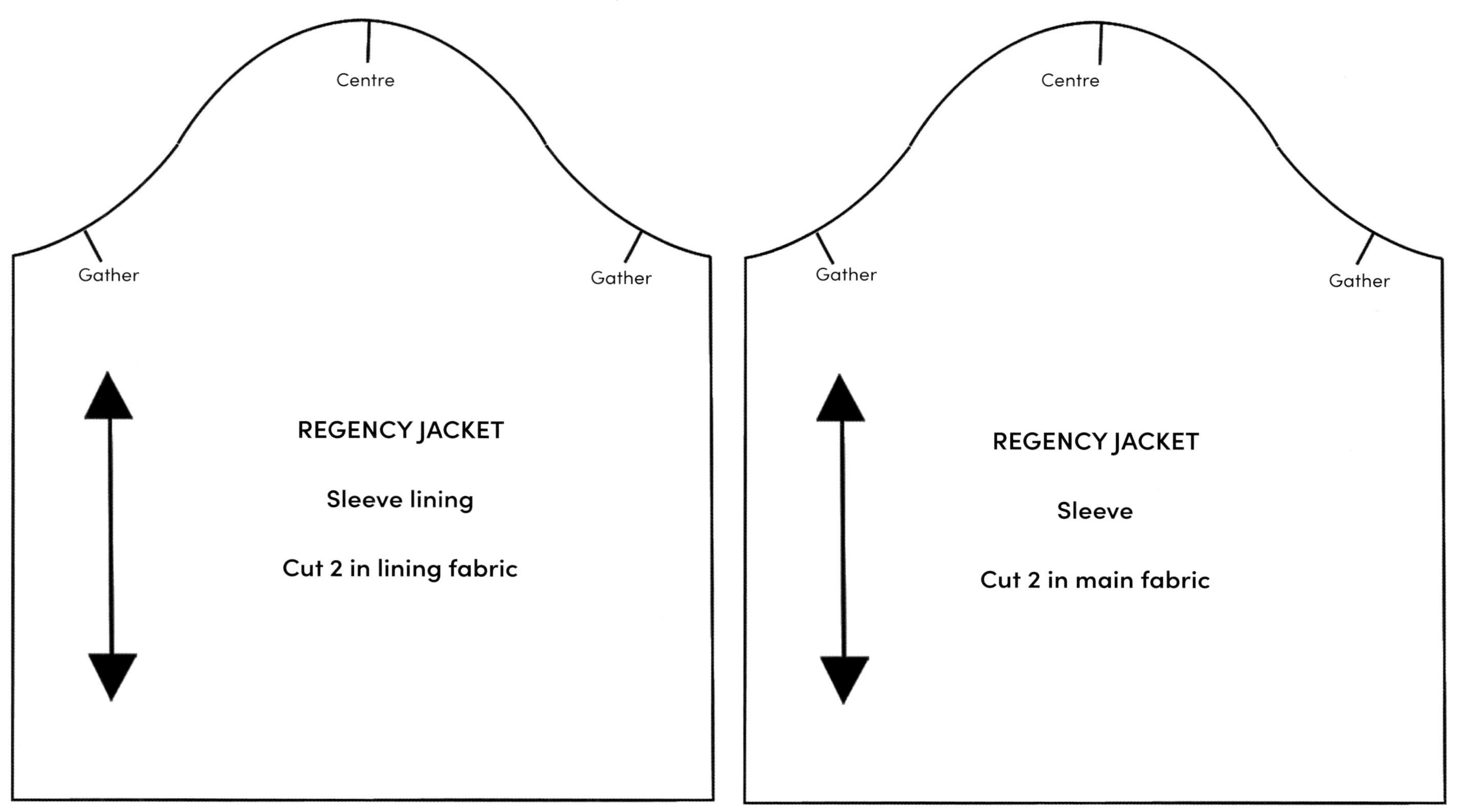
Centre
Gather
Gather
REGENCY JACKET
Sleeve lining
Cut 2 in lining fabric
Centre
Gather
Gather
REGENCY JACKET
Sleeve
Cut 2 in main fabric

SUPPLIERS

Choosing your fabric can be fun! For these projects, remember to think small and ditsy, lightweight cottons and woven fabric. Have a look in your fabric stash first - you may already have the perfect little gem tucked away. I love recycling fabric. Men's shirts are a good starting point, as the stripes and small checks work really well. We've designed a range of kits that have everything you need to make your project and takes the stress out of making choices.

They are available here :

Apple Blossom Gift Emporium

1B Parkside Works
Gotham Road
East Leake
Leicestershire
LE12 6JG

www.lillyrosedolls.uk

Claire has had a love affair with fabric all her life – at the age of four, she was designing dolly clothes from her mother's stash of off-cut fabrics. In 2020 Claire took a year out from running her busy Ragdoll business to play with fabric and Apple Blossom Wood came to life. With the range launching in 2023, it has been a whirlwind journey. Very exciting times are here, as Apple Blossom Wood now has a new home, Apple Bossom Gift Emporium, in the heart of England, where you will be able to buy all your supplies to make the boys and girls, patterns, kits and miniature haberdashery, as well as participate in regular workshops.

Claire lives in the heart of England in a small village, from which she takes her inspiration. She lives with her three children, three cats and a garden full of birds.

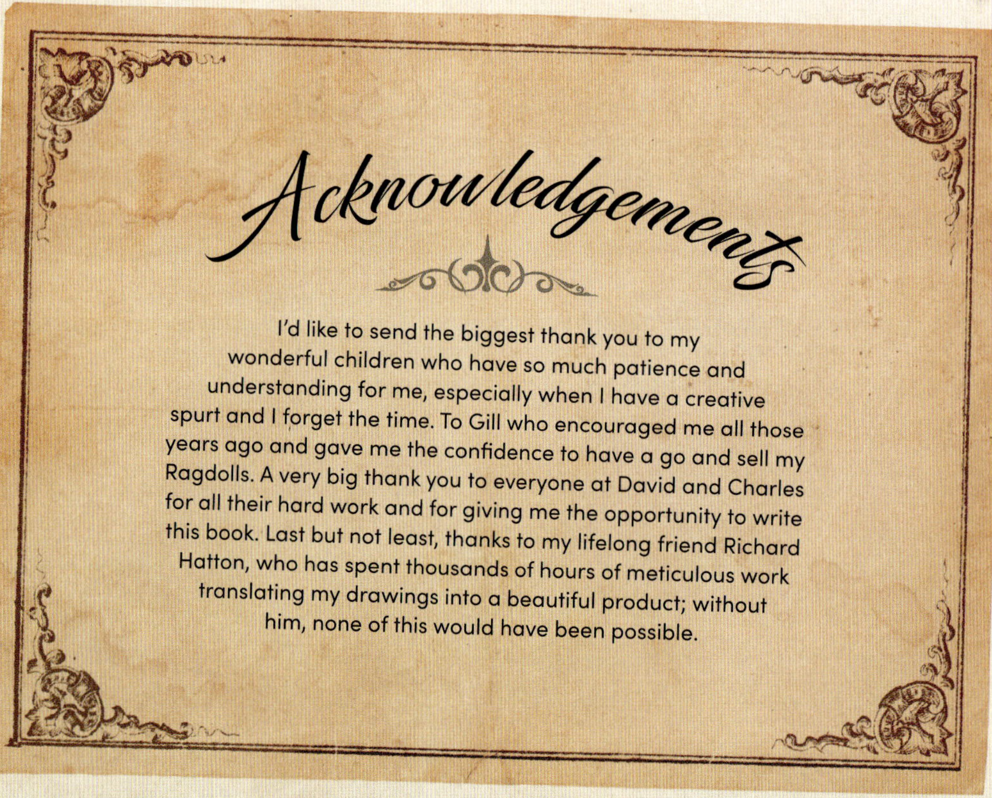

Acknowledgements

I'd like to send the biggest thank you to my wonderful children who have so much patience and understanding for me, especially when I have a creative spurt and I forget the time. To Gill who encouraged me all those years ago and gave me the confidence to have a go and sell my Ragdolls. A very big thank you to everyone at David and Charles for all their hard work and for giving me the opportunity to write this book. Last but not least, thanks to my lifelong friend Richard Hatton, who has spent thousands of hours of meticulous work translating my drawings into a beautiful product; without him, none of this would have been possible.

INDEX

animals 14–47
  fabrics 9
  templates 82–9
  universal 83–4
  see also clothing
appliqué 12
  apron dress with appliqué 39, 63, 102
arms 19–21, 83

back stitch 12
berry brim hat 38, 70–1, 109
Bertie Bear 6, 14, 16–23
  clothing 22–3, 49–56, 90–8
  templates 84–5
blanket stitch 12
bloomers, bella 30, 38, 44, 48, 64–5, 103
  ribbon bow variation 64–5
bodies 19–20, 83
buttons
  apron dress 61–2
  jacket 66–7, 72, 74
  shirt 50–1
  trouser 52–3, 77, 79
  waistcoat 49, 57–8, 75–6

cap, peaky 23, 36, 56, 98
Chester and Sapphire Foxes 32–9
  clothing 36–9, 68–74, 106–12
  templates 87
clothing 48–81
  for Bertie Bear 22–3, 49–56, 90–8
  for Chester and Sapphire Foxes 36–9, 68–74, 106–12
  for Eli and Elisha Elephants 28–31, 50–1, 57–67, 99–105
  for Emma and Byron Highland Cows 44–7, 75–81, 113–17
  fabrics 9, 48
  scale 9
  shaping 11
  templates 82, 90–117
coat, Shelby 23, 54–5, 96–7
cotton 9
cows see Emma and Byron Highland Cows
cutting out 10

darts 10–11, 82
  coat 54, 96
  jacket 59, 66, 80, 100, 105, 113, 116
  trouser 52, 77, 90, 114
  waistcoat 49, 58, 75, 90, 99
dresses, apron 31, 45, 48, 61–3, 102
  with appliqué 39, 63, 102

ears
  bear 21, 85
  cow 43
  elephant 27, 85
  fox 87
Eli and Elisha Elephants 24–31
  clothing 28–31, 50–1, 57–67, 99–105
  templates 85–6
Emma and Byron Highland Cows 40–7
  clothing 44–7, 75–81, 113–17
  fabrics 9
  templates 88–9

fabrics 9, 48
faces
  bear 21
  cow 43
  elephant 27
  fox 35
faux fur 9, 43
felt 9
foxes see Chester and Sapphire Foxes
fraying, prevention 10

gather stitch 12
gathering techniques 11

hand sewing 10, 12
hats
  berry brim hat 38, 70–1, 109
  peaky cap 23, 36, 56, 98
heads
  bear 19, 20, 84–5
  cow 42–3, 88–9
  elephant 26, 86
  fox 34–5, 87
highland cows see Emma and Byron Highland Cows
horns 43, 88

ironing 10

jackets
  Harris 37, 68–9, 106–8
  Josephine 31, 44, 66–7, 104–5
  perfect petal 39, 72–4, 110–12
  regency 46, 80–1, 116–17
  swallowtail 29, 59–60, 100–1

legs 19–21, 84

materials 8–9

pattern transfer 10
pincord (pinwale/needlecord) 9
pleats 11
pockets
  apron dress 61–2, 102
  coat 54, 96
  trouser 52–3, 77–9, 95, 115
  waistcoat 57–8, 99
pressing 10

running/gather stitch 12

scale, clothing 9
seam allowances 10
sewing kits 8
sewing machines 10
sewing technique 10
shaping 11
shirts 23, 28, 36, 50–1, 91–2
stitches, hand 12

tails, cow 43, 89
techniques 10–12
templates 10, 82–117
  animals 82–9
  clothing 82, 90–117
tools 8–9
transferring patterns 10
trousers 48
  classic 22, 29, 37, 52–3, 93–5
  Darcy 47, 77–9, 114–15

waistbands 53, 79, 95, 114
waistcoats 48
  Austen 22, 36, 49, 90
  horseshoe 28, 57–8, 99
  Mandarin 47, 75–6, 113
wardrobes see clothing
wool felt 9

A DAVID AND CHARLES BOOK

David and Charles is an imprint of David and Charles, Ltd
Suite A, Tourism House, Pynes Hill, Exeter, EX2 5WS

First published in the UK and USA in 2025

A catalogue record for this book is available from the British Library.

ISBN-13: 9781446314258 paperback
ISBN-13: 9781446314272 EPUB

This book has been printed on paper from approved suppliers and made from pulp from sustainable sources.

Printed in China through Asia Pacific Offset for:
David and Charles, Ltd
Suite A, Tourism House, Pynes Hill, Exeter, EX2 5WS

10 9 8 7 6 5 4 3 2 1

Publishing Director: Ame Verso
Senior Commissioning Editor: Sarah Callard
Publishing Manager: Jeni Chown
Editor: Victoria Allen
Project Editor: Sarah Hoggett
Lead Designer: Sam Staddon
Design: Anna Wade and Jess Pearson
Pre-press Designer: Susan Reansbury
Illustrations and Art Direction: Prudence Rogers
Photography: Jason Jenkins
Production Manager: Beverley Richardson

Layout of the digital edition of this book may vary depending on reader hardware and display settings.